Treating Incest:
A Multimodal Systems
Perspective

THE *JOURNAL OF PSYCHOTHERAPY & THE FAMILY* SERIES:

- *Computers and Family Therapy*

- *Divorce Therapy*

- *Family Therapy Education and Supervision*

- *Marriage and Family Enrichment*

- *Treating Incest: A Multimodal Systems Perspective*

- *Severe and Chronic Disorders: New Perspectives on the Family*

- *Minority Family Therapy*

- *Feminist Family Therapy*

Treating Incest: A Multimodal Systems Perspective

Terry S. Trepper
Mary Jo Barrett
Editors

The Haworth Press
New York • London

Treating Incest: A Multimodal Systems Perspective has also been published as *Journal of Psychotherapy & the Family*, Volume 2, Number 2, Summer 1986.

The Haworth Press, Inc., 28 East 22 Street, New York, NY 10010-6194
EUROSPAN/Haworth, 3 Henrietta Street, London WC2E 8LU England

Library of Congress Cataloging-in-Publication Data

Treating incest: a multimodal systems perspective.

   Bibliography: p.
   1. Sexually abused children. 2. Incest victims. I. Trepper, Terry S. II. Barrett, Mary Jo.
RJ507.S49T74   1986   618.92'89   86-4719
ISBN 0-86656-512-4

Treating Incest:
A Multimodal Systems
Perspective

Journal of Psychotherapy & the Family
Volume 2, Number 2

CONTENTS

PART II: TREATMENT OF INTRAFAMILY SEXUAL ABUSE

Acknowledgements

In this edition, we have attempted to combine both the theoretical and the clinical aspects of intrafamily child sexual abuse. In many respects, this reflects the collaboration between the research focus of the Family Studies Center at Purdue University Calumet, and the clinical focus of Midwest Family Resource. Our two groups had independently been developing similar theoretical and clinical approaches to treating intrafamily child sexual abuse without knowing of the work of the other. We are extremely grateful to Charles Figley for encouraging this "marriage" by suggesting the project and helping us see it through to completion.

We would like to thank the staff and students of the Family Studies Center, both past and present, for their contributions to this edition. We are particularly grateful to Bridgett Booker, Becky Lee, and Carolyn Cory, who served as research assistants. We are indebted to Linda Stone Fish for her meticulous review of the manuscript. Also, our gratitude goes to Patricia Geiger and Mary Moss for many hours of preparation and reparation of the manuscripts.

A special "thank you" should be given to the families we have treated. We have over the course of the years learned what love, compassion, and hope truly means from families who were told by others (and began to believe) that they had forfeited the right to be a family. We are certain, too, that these families would wish to thank the therapists at Midwest Family Resource, and Southlake Center for Mental Health, in Merrillville, IN, for helping them show that the reports of their family's demise was "greatly exaggerated."

Finally, a personal note of thanks is given to our spouses, Carolyn Trepper, and Dennis O'Keefe, for enduring the craziness that accompanies the obsessive-compulsive behavior of editing and writing for a special edition.

Treating Incest:
A Multimodal Systems
Perspective

EDITORIAL NOTE

The incidence of child sexual abuse in this country appears to be increasing and at a dramatic rate. The popular media have only recently discussed the wide-spread existence of this problem. Although clinical reports of incest have appeared in the practitioner literature for over thirty years, only recently have scholarly journals published systematic studies of this problem. As the editors point out in their introduction to this collection, the enactment of more stringent child abuse reporting laws nationwide and increased public education about the problem, there has been a dramatic increase in the need for incest-related psychotherapy. Few clinicians, however, feel prepared to handle these types of cases.

This collection, entitled *Treating Incest: A Multimodal Systems Perspective*, is the second issue in the *Journal of Psychotherapy & the Family*'s second volume. The aim of the Journal is to provide the most well-written, accurate, authoritative, and relevant information on critical issues in the practice of psychotherapy with families. This issue, consistent with the Journal's aim, intends to promote new insight into the complex problems associated with incest.

Though most psychotherapists, confronted with a case of incest, would prefer to send both victim and perpetrator to another who specializes in these cases, this collection should provide an important source of information about the assessment and treatment of the family. Such preparation, then, may encourage the clinician to provide at least some appropriate crisis intervention for the family or families involved. And if a referral is made, the clinician can make informed judgments about who should treat what when and under what circumstances.

The editors, Terry S. Trepper and Mary Jo Barrett, make an excellent team of editors. Each applies years of experience in this area. The former, a university professor, researcher and clinical educator, the latter, a director of one of the largest incest treatment centers in the country. They are among the very few systemically-oriented psychotherapists qualified to treat families affected by incest.

Terry S. Trepper is the Director of the Family Studies Center and Associate Professor of Psychology at Purdue University (Calumet). He is also the former director of the Human Sexuality Program and currently coordinating consultant to the Southlake Center Family Studies Program. He also has a private practice in Chicago. He has served as guest editor for another special issue by the *Journal of Sex Education and Therapy*. Dr. Trepper has presented scholarly papers at the annual conferences of all of the major national mental health associations and has developed a family treatment program for incest that is currently being used in a number of sites nationally.

Mary Jo Barrett is Director of the Midwest Family Resource Associates (Chicago) which has one of the largest case loads of incest families in the country. She is a member of the adjunct faculty of the Institute for Juvenile Research, University of Illinois, Chicago and field instructor for both the University of Illinois and the University of Chicago. She has presented numerous professional workshops on family abuse, including child sexual abuse, nationally and internationally. She has many years of experience with treating incest as a practitioner, clinical supervisor, and administrator.

This edited collection is a compliment to the editors' impressive credentials in this field. No other collection has included so many key individuals knowledgeable about family-centered treatment of incest.

Similar to the guest editors, Noel Larson and James Maddock have worked for many years with incest families and have trained thousands of professionals in understanding the family dynamics involved with incest. Howard Levy is the Chief of Pediatrics at Children's Memorial Hospital in Chicago, and, along with Stephen Sheldon, has developed an internationally known program for medically evaulating sexually abused children. David Finkelhor is an internationally known expert on the sociology of child abuse, and the recent author of *Child Sexual Abuse: New Theory and Research*. Ann Burgess is another internationally known scholar with expertise in several areas including child sexual abuse. Stephen Schweitzer and Robert Kurlychek are both forensic psychologists who have written and taught extensively on the courtroom process itself, and how therapists in family-related cases need to prepare for serving as expert witnesses. Finally, Jon Conte is a nationally recognized expert on social work with child sexual abuse cases, particularly in the area of theory development and public policy. Also, he is founding editor of the new journal, *The Journal of Family Violence and Abuse*.

Trepper and Barrett have skillfully assembled and organized this collection of papers into two complementary parts. Part I: Conceptual Framework for the Assessment of Intrafamily Sexual Abuse, includes four chapters which provide various methods of conceptualizing the problem of incest. Part II: Treatment of Intrafamily Sexual Abuse, includes five chapters which articulate various methods and approaches to assessment and treatment.

The central theme of the collection, according to Trepper and Barrett, is that effective treatment of incest requires a systemic approach. Such an approach views incestuous activity as the *product* of a problematic family system, rather than the cause. Moreover, this approach sees *all* family members as sharing in both the development and maintenance of the problem. At the same time, however, the editors and their contributors are sensitive to individual, personality/behavioral dynamics of the family members, though the unit of treatment is the family system.

Thus, a *multiple systems* perspective monitors and modifies *all* systems involved, including the larger ecosystems (e.g., environmental or community conditions), as well as the family and its members. This approach is in stark contrast to the prevailing approaches which view incest as primarily the result of *individual factors* associated with the perpetrator or victim. The purpose of the collection, then, is to provide practitioners with the state-of-the-art approaches to assessing and treating incestuous families from a *multiple* systems perspective.

The Journal is dedicated to improving the arts and sciences of psychotherapy practice by focusing on the family and its role in the prevention, development and maintenance of psychopathology. When the incest is detected within the system all members are affected in varying degrees and with varying consequences. Psychotherapists called upon to intervene with incestuous families are in a key position to stop the pain and correct the problem, or make the problem worse. We hope that this collection, with its focus on assessment and treatment of the family system, will become a key reference for these psychotherapists and those who will be similarly challenged in the future.

C. R. Figley, Ph.D.
Editor

Introduction

Terry S. Trepper
Mary Jo Barrett

The number of reported cases of intrafamily child sexual abuse has increased dramatically during the past five years. This is due, in part, to the enactment of stricter child abuse reporting laws nationwide and increased public awareness of the problem. As a result, the mental health field is currently being inundated with requests by local protective service agencies and families themselves for treatment. This condition has put much pressure on the mental health community in general, and family therapists in particular, to develop expertise in a short period of time. The results, however, have been less than satisfactory. Many clinicians complain that even with the many articles, books, and training workshops that have recently proliferated, there is still a need for both theoretically sound and highly practical information on the assessment and treatment of incest.[1]

Because of the serious nature of these cases, therapists treating incest families are plagued by concerns which rarely present themselves with other problem areas. Questions that must be answered during the course of therapy include: (1) Is the family able to protect the child from further abuse during the course of therapy? (2) Should either the abusing parent or the abused child be removed from the home during the course of therapy, or is it in the best interest of all for the family to remain living together? (3) Who is the therapeutic unit of focus, the victim, perpetrator, or the entire family? (4) Should the treatment goal be to merely reduce the likelihood of further abuse, or should it address the myriad of problems with which most incest families present, and which may have contributed to the abuse? and (5) At what point can therapy be terminated?

Terry S. Trepper is the Director of the Family Studies Center and Associate Professor of Psychology at Purdue University Caulmet. He also has a private practice in Chicago.

Mary Jo Barrett is Director of the Midwest Family Resource Associates (Chicago). She is a member of the adjunct faculty of the Institute for Juvenile Research, University of Illinois, Chicago, and field instructor for both the University of Illinois and the University of Chicago.

[1]In this edition, *intrafamily sexual abuse*, and *incest* will be used interchangeably, and will mean any acts perpetrated on a child by an adult relative or paramour residing in or near the home, with the intention of sexually arousing the adult or the child. Also, unless otherwise noted, our examples will refer to father/daughter or step-father/step-daughter because it is the most commonly seen by family therapists.

PROBLEMS ASSOCIATED WITH THE TREATMENT OF INTRAFAMILY SEXUAL ABUSE

Besides these important questions, a number of unique problems are associated with clinically assessing and treating intrafamily child sexual abuse cases with which the therapist must be concerned. Some of these problems, if unsolved, will seriously hamper our ability to effectively manage these cases. The problem areas include, but are not limited to: the degree to which the values of the therapist affects treatment planning; the differing effects of an individual vs. a family focus on therapy outcome; the myriad of factors which may contribute to the occurrence of incest; the inadequacy of the assessment devices available; and the inadequacy of training for therapists working with incest families.

Values of the Therapist

One of the least discussed aspects of treatment of intrafamily sexual abuse is that of the values of the clinician or caseworker. Most students of the therapeutic process are in agreement that the therapist's values surrounding a problem will affect the nature of the therapy he or she provides (Corey, 1977). Given the degree of emotionality typically surrounding incestuous behavior, there is a great likelihood that the therapist's values and sentiment concerning the families and their behavior will intrude upon rational analysis (Trepper and Traicoff, 1983). What is unfortunate is that, due to the generally high level of family dysfunction present, it is these very cases that require the greatest amount of rationality for effective treatment.

There are a number of values-related issues with which a clinician must grapple. One obvious issue is whether or not parent-child incest is always harmful to the victim and/or family, and concomitantly can it ever be veiwed as a positive experience. Although most would agree with Finkelhor (1979; 1984) that sex between children and adults is wrong in any social and moral analysis, there certainly are cases, for example, where the sexual activity may be less traumatic than the breaking up of the family that often follows its disclosure.

A related concern is the level of anger a therapist may feel toward the family. Whereas family therapists are taught early in training to be aware of "interface issues" which may interfere with effective treatment (Bowen, 1978), case managers working with incest families often feel a great sense of hostility toward the perpetrator and the mother (Dietz and Craft, 1980). Often this interface problem is complicated by the clinician having been a sex-abuse victim as a child. It may be that a therapist, like the public in general, cannot intellectually defend against the breaking of two very strong cultural taboos at the same time, incest and pedophilia.

Whatever the reasons, and as understandable as they may be, the unquestioned holding of these values concerning the family will certainly interfere with an accurate assessment and treatment.

Individual vs. Family Focus

Whether the clinician views the intrafamily sexual abuse as primarily a result of *individual* factors, (e.g. a criminal or deranged act of the perpetrator), or *family* factors (e.g. the incest serving a family homeostatic function) will of course be reflected in the assessment style and treatment process (MacFarlane and Bulkley, 1982). Not surprisingly, therapists are usually divided by clinical and professional orientation.

From an individual focus, the so-called *victim-perpetrator* model continues to be the most commonly used way of conceptualizing incest for both the general public and clinicians alike (Rosenfeld, 1979). In this linear model, incest is seen as the aggressive act of a pathological or deviant adult perpetrator, against an innocent or uninvolved victim. This model evolved from traditional psychotherapy and the child advocacy movement (Conte, 1982), and has maintained a popularity in spite of its limitations.

There are a number of reasons the victim-perpetrator model is as popular as it is. First, as Rosenfeld (1979) points out, there is obvious truth to a model that proposes a child, being unable to cognitively give meaningful informed consent, should not be encouraged to have sex with an adult family member in whom the child must place ultimate trust. The second reason the victim-perpetrator conceptualizations are popular is that the model is simple; it is linear, directional, and intuitive. There is a natural tendency for all of us to try and make complex situations simple, and intrafamily child sexual abuse is no exception. The third reason is that the model allows us to keep a certain psychological distance from the behavior in question. If we can believe that only "sick" or deviant people commit such acts, the chance of us "normal" people becoming perpetrators is far less.

The second model, family systems, views incestuous activity as the product of a problematic family system rather than as the cause, and sees all family members as sharing in its development; that is, all family members are both victims and perpetrators (Straus, 1973; Trepper and Traicoff, 1985). Primarily supported by family therapists and many caseworkers, the systems view takes into account the havoc raised by families who are broken up, and provides a theoretical position for those sensitive to being thought of as professional "child stealers" (Finkelhor, 1984). Unfortunately, in their zeal to focus on the complexities of the family, workers assessing and treating primarily from a systems framework may miss important individual dynamics essential for understanding a particular case.

Clinicians who assess and treat from only a victim-perpetrator or systems view may, by virtue of their prejudice, miss many important factors necessary for a complete understanding of the individuals and family involved. This can only lead to incomplete therapy at best.

Multiple and Contradictory Dimensions of Assessment

Even when one has an adequate underlying causal view of intrafamily child sexual abuse upon which to base treatment, trying to decide which factors are important to focus upon is a monumental task. The literature is replete with "causal variables" for incest, from either the victim-perpetrator or systems view, and many times these views are contradictory. Only a partial list is possible here.

Incest fathers have been described as possessing little impulse control (Summit and Kryso, 1978), but at the same time being rigid and overcontrolled (Panton, 1979); a few have stated that the incest reflects a role confusion, where the father subconsciously confuses the daughter with his wife at a younger age (Justice and Justice, 1979; Summit and Kryso, 1978) or even with his mother, with whom he has never fully resolved Oedipal feelings (Gordon, 1955), though Frude (1982) argues the incest reflects a *direct* sexual interest in the daughter. Meiselman (1978) believes incest fathers are emotionally deprived from their families of origin, while Gebhard et al. (1965) found that true only for incest fathers where the child was a preadolescent. One writer sees precipitating factors, such as returning home from a long trip or the loss of a wife, as the most significant (Batten, 1983). Many writers suggest that an authoritarian personality plays a role and that physical violence is commonly present (Hermand and Hirschman, 1981), but others are far more tentative in that finding (Justice and Justice, 1979; Julian and Mohr, 1979). And many writers suggest that alcohol abuse by the perpetrator, if not the cause of intrafamily sexual abuse, plays a significant role in its expression (Maisch, 1973; Virkkunen, 1974). We agree with Renshaw (1982) that the descriptions of incest fathers are often contradictory and have little consensus in the literature.

A number of speculations concerning the mothers and daughters have also been made. For example, incest daughters have been described by most (e.g., Justice and Justice, 1979; Meiselman, 1978; Frude, 1982) as having poor relationships with their mothers, having a low self-esteem, needing attention, and being attractive. Many also have suggested a kind of seductiveness, but are quick to point out that if that occurs it is due to the inappropriate sexual behavior of the father (Summit and Kryso, 1978). Other factors mentioned by some include promiscuity, position in the family, and an unresolved Electra complex (Justice and Justice, 1979; Meiselman, 1978). Mothers have been described as deprived emotionally from their own family backgrounds, passive and dependent, weak and submissive, emotionally absent from the family, and either adverse to sex or promiscuous (Justice and Justice, 1979; Meiselman, 1978).

There are also many speculative descriptions in the literature of the family dynamics involved. Some have focused on the descriptive pathology of families, and have noted such predisposing factors as previous incest of the father or mother (e.g., Rosenfeld, 1979; Renshaw, 1982; Will, 1983); newly constituted families (Finkelhor, 1980); strong patriarchy present (Will, 1983); poor marital relationships (Giaretto, 1978) and poor mother-daughter relationships (Meiselman, 1978). Also noted is a disrupted or dysfunctional sexual relationship between father and mother (Renshaw, 1981), or a level of hypersexuality or family promiscuity (Weinberg, 1955).

Others have focused on the interactional nature of the family system. Terms such as functional (Bagley, 1969) and endogamic (Rosenfeld, 1979) incest have been used to describe family systems where the abuse is seen as serving family homeostasis (e.g., Kaufman et al., 1954; Machoka, 1967; Kennedy and Cormier, 1969; Straus, 1973; Rist, 1979; Renvoize, 1982). There has been little agreement, however, on the exact mechanisms involved. For example, does incestuous behavior occur where the "boundaries" are diffuse and no one knows or acts upon their formal roles? Or are the boundaries so rigid that a formal patriarchy can turn into a situation where a father feels he can dominate his daughter completely, including sexually?

A variety of environmental dimensions have been hypothesized as contributing to intrafamily sexual abuse as well. These include stress (Renshaw, 1982); social isolation; opportunity factors (Finkelhor, 1978); and an overriding male supremacy tolerated by our culture as a whole (Herman and Hirschman, 1977).

The larger number and often contradictory nature of the hypothesized dimensions make understanding the *causes* of incest expression extremely difficult. Part of the problem may be that the descriptions are usually not based on empirical findings but clinical observations of small samples. When they are data based, it is often from retrospective surveys of adult women victims (Conte, 1982). More likely, however, is that the myriad of descriptors may *all* be correct for some families in some situations.

Inadequate Assessment Devices

There are currently no instruments with which we are familiar that can provide the clinician with a measure of an individual or family's predisposition to intrafamily child sexual abuse. Neither are there tools designed specifically to provide information which will aid directly in the development of treatment plans for incest cases, although Tierney and Corwin (1983) suggest how specific information and devices may be used to develop such scales in the future. What is particularly needed is a measure of individual and family structural characteristics which would not only provide diagnostic information but permit an objective measure of individual and systemic change as a result of therapy.

Inadequate Training of Clinicians

One of the most common concerns heard by clinicians is that they are inadequately trained to deal with incest families, either in terms of assessment or treatment (Dietz and Craft, 1980). Family therapists do not typically focus on the assessment of individuals which may be critical in these cases (Finkelhor, 1984), but individually trained clinicians such as psychologists (who often do the assessment in an agency setting) rarely will incorporate family measures in their evaluation battery. It is clear that any clinician, regardless of his or her discipline or orientation, needs to be well versed in the complexities of intrafamily sexual abuse and design their assessment and treatment procedures accordingly.

PURPOSE OF THIS EDITION

This brief review suggests there are a number of questions which need to be answered and problems which need to be addressed for the effective treatment of intrafamily child sexual abuse. It is the intent of this edition to provide for the therapist working with cases of intrafamily child sexual abuse both a theoretical background in and practical information for the treatment of incest. In doing so, we wish to broaden the views of individually oriented clinicians beyond a victim-perpetrator approach to incest. At the same time, we wish to broaden the views of systems-oriented clinicians to think in terms of *all* systems involved, including individual and larger eco-systems. Only then can therapists fully understand and treat intrafamily child sexual abuse.

To accomplish this task, we have assembled a number of articles written by specialists in intrafamily child sexual abuse. At all times we have kept in mind the practicing clinician who is in need of specific and practical information in assessing and treating incest families. Even articles that lean more toward the theoretical should provide the therapist with a clearer understanding of the intricate interactive dynamics involved, so as to ultimately result in more effective therapy.

We have informally divided the edition into two sections. The first focuses on assessment issues. Trepper and Barrett's article provides an integrative framework to assessing intrafamily sexual abuse, incorporating individual, family systems, and eco-systems into a clinical evaluation. Larson and Maddock's paper provides a functional typology of incest families with specific suggestions for incorporating this into an assessment scheme. Levy and Sheldon's article demonstrates how important it is to integrate medicine with family assessment and how the medical field can be included in psychological and family assessment of intrafamily child sexual abuse. David Finkelhor's excellent paper on the four preconditions to child abuse reminds family therapists that the role of the perpetrator must be acknowledged. And finally, Hartman and Burgess gives us a powerful and complete description of the child-victim experience before, during, and after the abuse.

The second section of the edition focuses on treatment issues and techniques. Barrett and her colleagues provide an overview of a successful model for the treatment of intrafamily child sexual abuse which addresses ecosystems, family structure, and individual components. Trepper's article on the apology session gives the clinician a powerful, specific intervention to use early in therapy. Schweitzer and Kurlychek offers a practical guide for family therapists giving court testimony in cases of intrafamily child sexual abuse. Finally, Jon Conte provides a synthesis of the state-of-the-art in the assessment and treatment of intrafamily child sexual abuse, and offers suggestions for the future in research and clinical practice.

It is hoped that this edition will challenge the reader. The articles presented represent many theoretical views, from individual-analytical to family-systems. The skilled therapist should be able to draw upon material from these differing sources and accommodate these into his or her own work. We hope the material presented herein will begin making the assessment and treatment of intrafamily child sexual abuse an easier and less perplexing task for the family therapist.

REFERENCES

Bagley, C. (1969). Incest behavior and the incest taboo. *Social Problems*, 16, 505–519.
Batten, D. A. (1983). Incest: A review of the literature. *Medical and Scientific Law*, 23, 245–253.
Bowen, M. (1978). *Family therapy in clinical practice*. New York: Jason Aronson.
Corey, G. (1977). *Theory and practice of counseling and psychotherapy*. Monterey, CA: Brooks/Cole.
Conte, J. (1982). Sexual abuse of children: Enduring questions for social work. In Jon R. Conte and David A. Shore (Eds.), *Social work and child sexual abuse*, New York: Haworth Press.
Dietz, C. A., and Craft, J. L. (1980). Family dynamics of incest: A new perspective. *Social Casework*, 61, 602–609.
Finkelhor, D. (1978). Psychological, cultural, and structural factors in incest and family sexual abuse. *Journal of Marriage and Family Counseling*, 4, 45–50.
Finkelhor, D. (1979). What's wrong with sex between adults and children? *American Journal of Orthopsychiatry*, 49, 692–697.

Finkelhor, D. (1980). Risk factors in the sexual victimization of children. *Child abuse and neglect*, 4, 265–273.

Finkelhor, D. (1984). *Child sexual abuse*. New York: The Free Press.

Frude, N. (1982). The sexual nature of sexual abuse: A review of the literature. *Child Abuse and Neglect*, 6, 211–223.

Gebhard, P. H., et al., (1965). *Sex offenders; An Analysis of types*. New York: Harper and Row.

Giaretto, H. (1978). Humanistic treatment of father-daughter incest. *Journal of Humanistic Psychology*, 18.

Gordon, L. (1955). Incest as revenge against the pre-oedipal mother. *Psychoanalytic Review*, 42, 284–292.

Herman, J., and Hirschman, L. (1977). Father-daughter incest. *Signs*, 4, 735–756.

Herman, J., and Hirschman, L. (1981). Families at risk for father-daughter incest. *American Journal of Psychiatry*, 138, 967–970.

Julian, V., and Mohr, C. (1979). Father-daughter incest: Profile of the offender. *Victimology; An International Journal*, 4.

Justice, B., and Justice, R. (1979). *The broken taboo: Sex in the family*. New York: Human Sciences Press.

Kaufman, I., Peck, A. L., and Tagiuri, C. K. (1954). The family constellation and overt incestuous relations between father and daughter. *American Journal of Orthopsychiatry*, 24, 266–277.

Kennedy, M., and Cormier, B. M. (1969). Father-daughter incest: Treatment of the family. *Laval Medical*, 40, 946–950.

Machoka, P., Pittman, F. S., and Flomenhaft, K. (1967). Incest as a family affair. *Family Process*, 6, 98–116.

Maisch, H. (1973). *Incest*. London: Andre Deutsch.

MacFarlane, K., and Bulkley, J. (1982). Treating child sexual abuse: An overview of current program models. In J. Conte and D. Shore (Eds.), *Social work and child sexual abuse*. New York: Haworth Press.

Meiselman, K. C. (1978). *Incest*. San Francisco: Jossey-Bass.

Panton, J. H. (1979). MMPI profile configurations associated with incestuous and non-incestuous child molesting. *Psychological Reports*, 45, 335–338.

Renshaw, D. (1982). *Incest: Understanding and treatment*. Boston: Little, Brown.

Renvoize, J. (1982). *Incest: A family pattern*. London: Routledge and Kegan Paul.

Rist, K. (1979). Incest; Theoretical and clinical views. *American Journal of Orthopsychiatry*, 49, 630–691.

Rosenfeld, A. (1979). Endogamic incest and the victim-perpetrator model. *American Journal of Diseases of Children*, 133, 406–410.

Straus, M. (1973). A general systems theory approach to a theory of violence between family members. *Social Science Information*, 12, 105–125.

Summit, R., and Kryso, J. (1978). Sexual abuse of children: A clinical spectrum. *American Journal of Orthopsychiatry*, 48, 237–251.

Tierney, K. J., and Corwin, D. L. (1983). Exploring intrafamilial child sexual abuse: A systems approach. In David Finkelhor et al (Eds.), *The dark side of families*. Beverly Hills: Sage.

Trepper, T. S., and Traicoff, E. M. (1983). Treatment of intrafamily sexuality: Issues in therapy and research. *Journal of Sex Education and Therapy*, 9, 14–18.

Trepper, T. S., and Traicoff, E. M. (1985). Treatment of intrafamily sexuality: Conceptual rationale and model for family therapy. *Journal of Sex Education and Therapy*, in press.

Virkkunen, M. (1974). Incest offenses and alcoholism. *Medical and Scientific Law*, 14, 124.

Weinburg, S. K. (1955). *Incest behavior*, New York: Citadel.

Will, D. (1983). Approaching the incestuous and sexually abusive family. *Journal of Adolescence*, 6, 229–246.

PART I: CONCEPTUAL FRAMEWORK FOR THE ASSESSMENT OF INTRAFAMILY SEXUAL ABUSE

Vulnerability to Incest: A Framework for Assessment

Terry S. Trepper
Mary Jo Barrett

One of the first tasks in the treatment of intrafamily child sexual abuse is the development of an appropriate assessment scheme by which a family can be evaluated. Without such a scheme, the therapist is unable to adequately assess the complex web of factors typically present in most incest families, nor develop an effective treatment plan.

The purpose of this paper is to present a conceptual framework for assessing the multiple dimensions of intrafamily sexual abuse. For our purposes, the term "intrafamily sexual abuse" is used interchangeably with "incest," and refers to cases involving parent and child, or step-parent and step-child sexuality. Also, unless otherwise noted, we will be referring to father and daughter or step-father and step-daughter incest, although we feel our assessment model applies to any sexual abuse within the nuclear family. We purposely limit our discussion to *intra*family sexuality because, practically speaking, these are the cases which by far present most often to clinicians working in the field, not because other forms of child sexual abuse are unimportant nor have a profound impact on the family. And although the assessment framework may be general-

Terry S. Trepper is the Director of the Family Studies Center and Associate Professor of Psychology at Purdue University Calumet. He also has a private practice in Chicago.

Mary Jo Barrett is Director of the Midwest Family Resource Associate (Chicago). She is a member of the adjunct faculty of the Institute for Juvenile Research, University of Illinois, Chicago, and field instructor for both the University of Illinois and the University of Chicago.

izable to *extra*familial sexual abuse, we feel that sex within the family, particularly parent-child, does indeed represent a "special case" of sexual abuse which needs to be studied in its own context.

VULNERABILITY: A FRAMEWORK FOR ASSESSING INTRAFAMILY SEXUAL ABUSE

The assessment model presented in the following pages, although not empirically based, is pragmatic in its approach. This model has been extremely useful in our combined work with hundreds of incest families over the last five years in the Chicago and Northwest Indiana area. Although it is primarily a guide for a focused assessment and treatment plan development, this framework may also be useful as a conceptual base for future research into the nature of intrafamily sexual abuse.

To develop our assessment model, we took into account two realities. First, previous unidimensional models have proven incomplete in explaining intrafamily sexual abuse (Tierney and Corwin, 1983; Conte, 1982). To assess only one dimension, for example the psychopathology of the perpetrator, would be at best incomplete. Second, there is a convergence by writers in the field upon similar descriptions of the factors contributing to incest. Even though many of these clinical descriptors are contradictory (cf. Renshaw, 1982), most likely each is seeing at least a partial component of the "cause" incest. That is, each of these descriptors are correct for some families at some time. Therefore, we wanted to build an assessment model which took all possible contributing factors into account in an organized fashion.

Some writers have recently hypothesized multiple factors contributing to the development of family physical abuse (e.g., Garbriano, 1977; Gelles, 1980; Straus, 1980), and family sexual abuse (e.g., Finkelhor, 1978; Tierney and Corwin, 1983). Our framework, however, is more akin to the vulnerability (Zubin and Spring, 1977; Gottschalk, 1983) or diathesis-stress (Rosenthal, 1971) models increasingly popular in the field of abnormal psychology. These models state that the goal of assessment should not be to isolate the one underlying cause of a disorder, but to identify how *vulnerable* a person or system is based on many possible contributing factors. At that point the likelihood of *expression* of the disorder based on the presence of precipitating situations may be more accurately assessed.

The underlying premise of our vulnerability model is as follows: There is no cause of intrafamily sexual abuse. Instead, all families are endowed with a degree of *vulnerability* based on individual, family, and environmental factors, which may express as incest *if* a precipitating event takes place *and* the family's coping skills are low. Although there are many possible factors contributing to a family's vulnerability, the factors described in the following section seems to encompass at least the most commonly hypothesized components.

VULNERABILITY FACTORS

Our model is utilized not only as assessment but also as an ongoing therapeutic tool. Initially, the clinician observes the individual, family, and dyadic interactions based on the vulnerability factors listed below. From these observations, the therapist develops a treatment plan that addresses each of the different factors and their influence upon each other. Interventions then are designed to interrupt the dysfunctional sequences that had previously been established within the family's context.

Family of Origin
of Father and Mother

The family of origin of the perpetrator and spouse is viewed by many as contributing to the vulnerability of intrafamily sexual abuse. The parenting and marital styles in incestuous families are cyclical in nature, meaning that if a father or mother were an incest victim, or came from a family where incest occurred, there is an increased likelihood of incest in this family (Rosenfeld, 1979; Renshaw, 1982; Will, 1983). This happens even if surprisingly the abuse were violent or a frightening experience for the parent when it occurred. Other factors include the degree of emotional deprivation or neglect the parent experienced as a child, the expression of conditional love by his or her parents, and whether or not there was abandonment in their family, either actual or emotional (Justice and Justice, 1979; Meiselman, 1978).

During our individual diagnostic sessions, we ask specific direct questions about the parents' own family. These questions focus on the parents experience as children with respect their own abuse, the degree of emotional deprivation or abandonment (including the swings between this and overinvolvement), the expression of conditional love, the style of discipline, and the occurrence of physical abuse. We attempt whenever possible to corroborate the information by having sessions with the extended family.

Personality Factors of Family Members

In evaluating the individual and personality characteristics of the parents and child, we are actually assessing two aspects. First, we evaluate the personality characteristics or psychopathology that may have contributed to the occurrence and maintenance of the incestuous behavior. At the same time, we attempt to assess the impact of the sexual abuse on the individual's psychological functioning. For the father, these would include the degree of sociopathic characteristics, such as lack of impulse control, the need for immediate gratification, and lack of guilt (Summit and Kryso, 1978); the degree of dominance and aggressiveness (Herman and Herschman, 1981); the presence of sexual disorder, particularly secondary erectile dysfunction (Renshaw, 1982); and the need for constant love and adoration (Meiselman, 1978). Of course the presence of obvious psychopathology, such as psychosis, may contribute to vulnerability.

Because we view all members of the family as being involved at some level in intrafamily sexual abuse, we individually assess other family members besides the perpetrator. For the mother, we evaluate the degree of passivity, dependence, and poor self-esteem, along with possible sexual dysfunction such as inhibited sexual desire (Justice and Justice, 1978; Meiselman, 1978). For the daughter we evaluate the degree of passivity, dependence, and sociopathy. In no way, of course, do we suggest the daughter *caused* her own abuse; we instead are interested in the daughter's individual personality characteristics which may need to change to help ensure no further abuse takes place.

We use both objective and projective personality tests, along with clinical interviews, in our individual evaluations. The MMPI is used to provide information on possible psychopathology, such as sociopathy and depression, and general personality characteristics such as passivity, dependence, and introversion. The TAT is used to provide information on self-esteem, perceptions of role within the family, and need for and ability to provide nurturance. Finally, the Purdue Sexuality Questionnaire[1] is used with the parents to obtain detailed information on sexual attitudes, behaviors, and possible dysfunctions.

Family System Factors

There are three levels of systemic functioning which is evaluated as possibly contributing to a family's vulnerability: family style, family structure, and communication patterns. *Family style* may be defined as pervasive and enduring patterns of interaction a family displays. *Family structure* refers to the organization of a family with regard to roles, hierarchies, rules, and power (Minuchin, 1974). *Family communication patterns* refers to the degree of the clarity and directness of various forms of communication, including verbal and non-verbal.

Family styles most vulnerable to incest have been outlined by Larson and Maddox (1984) and include the following: (1) *Affection Seeking*, which is characterized by a great amount of affection exchange, seduction, positive intent, and object connection; (2) *Pansexual*, characterized by oversexualization of their sexual patterns, where the family is closest when being sexual either openly or symbolically; (3) *Hostile-Negative*, which is characterized by a family pattern of displacing anger, a desire to hurt each other, and where anger and sexuality are paired; and (4) *Violent Rape*, where the entire family is organized toward violence, often paranoid, and with flimsy reality testing. Even though the second two styles are the most stereotypic, 94% of Larson and Maddox's population fall into the first two categories.

There are a variety of ways family therapists have conceptualized *family structure*. One model which we have found useful is Olson's Circumplex (see Figure 1), as it offers both a theoretical framework and assessment instruments with which to work (Olson et al., 1982). In this model two interacting dimensions, cohesion and adaptability, are used to describe family behavior. *Cohesion* assesses the degree to which family members are separated or connected emotionally to one another, and is displayed as a continuum from disengaged to enmeshed. *Adaptability* assesses the extent to which a family is flexible and adaptable to change, and is displayed on a continuum from rigid to chaotic.

Families most vulnerable to the development of incest can be present in any of the extreme ranges, but most often appear rigid and enmeshed or chaotic and enmeshed. In the former case, the family has a strict hierarchical nature, with inflexible rules and stereotypic sex roles; in the latter case, family rules change constantly, formal roles fluctuate so to become inappropriate, and the family experiences a feeling of being leaderless. In both cases, the family is isolated from or suspicious of others, looks to itself to satisfy individuals' emotional needs, and rallies when outsiders threaten the sanctity of the system.

A family structure classification more specific to intrafamily sexual abuse was developed by Barrett and her associates, and is based upon the structural family therapy model (Minuchin, 1974; 1981). Most clinicians have narrowly focused on the mother-daughter role reversal as the primary incongruent hierarchy that maintains incestuous relationships. Unfortunately, this view neglects many family hierarchical structures that also maintain and promote intrafamily sexual abuse. The following descriptions, shown in Figure 2, exemplify some of the most common family structures found in those vulnerable to incest:

Father Executive: This commonly seen structure shows the father as the executive in the system, and the daughter reversing roles with mother who is either emotionally or physically absent from the family. Mother may be seen as "one of the children," but more commonly has withdrawn from the family emotionally. The daughter in this structure assumes the responsibilities heretofore provided by the mother, including

FIGURE 1. CIRCUMPLEX MODEL: SIXTEEN TYPES OF MARITAL AND FAMILY SYSTEMS

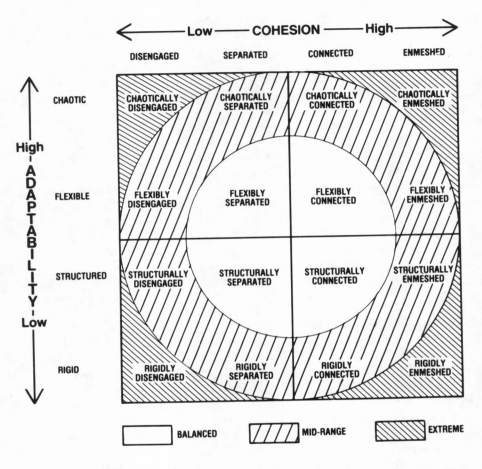

child-care for younger siblings, and emotional and sexual closeness with her father. This structure occurs most often in families with dominant-aggressive fathers, with fairly rigid and stereotyped views of male-female relationships.

Mother Executive: This structure is most commonly found among step-families and paramours, although not exclusively. The mother is the sole executive, and the father finds himself functioning in many respects as one of the children; that is, has little parental responsibility, and in fact is "parented" by the mother. His needs, sometimes sexual, are then met by a daughter who is actually a generational peer. The daughter in this family may also take on many of the co-executive functioning.

Fig. 2. Family structures in intrafamily child sexual abuse

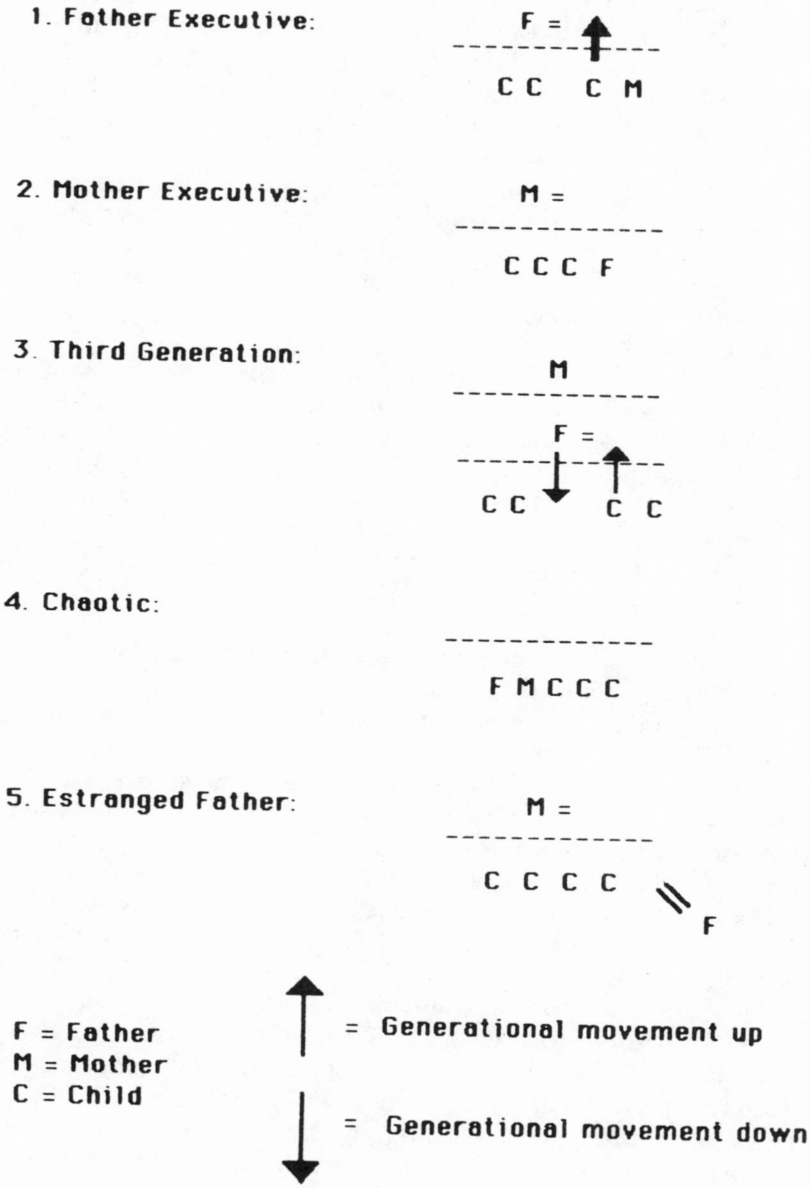

1. Father Executive:

F =

– – – – – – – –⬆️– – –

C C   C M

2. Mother Executive:

M =

– – – – – – – – – – –

C C C F

3. Third Generation:

M

– – – – – – – – – – –

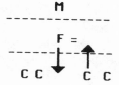

F =

– – – – – –⬇️– –⬆️– – –

C C   C C

4. Chaotic:

– – – – – – – – – – –

F M C C C

5. Estranged Father:

M =

– – – – – – – – – – –

C C C C   ⫽

F

F = Father
M = Mother
C = Child

⬆️ = Generational movement up

⬇️ = Generational movement down

Third Generation: In this structure we find the mother reacting and interacting in the same manner and style as a third generation, or grandparent. She parents the executive father, but has a more polar relationship with the children. She is at times very removed and distant, more like a family observer; at other times she moves in closely and with great executive force. The daughter, again, will then function as the "wife" in her mother's absence but like a daughter in her presence. The father then will fluctuate between the parental and sibling subsystem.

Chaotic: This structure is one in which there is functionally *no* executive subsystem present or typically available. The parents and children function on the same level with regard to their formal roles, and no one enforces the rules or boundaries. Emotionally, this structure finds most members of the family showing immature judgement, displaying little impulse control and expressing the need for immediate gratification. The father and daughter's sexual behavior looks actually like sibling sexual exploration.

Family communication is the final family component we examine in assessing vulnerability. Conflict avoidance, secretiveness, hostility, and double-binding communication patterns are commonly present in sexually abusing families. Dysfunctional communication patterns between the father and mother are quite common, and often lead to avoidance between the two. This same pattern may unfortunately exist between mother and daughter as well. We have found these families to be lacking in the ability to communicate affectively, while maintaining effective instrumental communication.

The family systems factors mentioned above is assessed in a number of ways. Usually *family style* is apparent through direct observation and questions during interviews. Most families fall into the "affection-seeking" and "pansexual" style, and these families are the most amenable to treatment. The "hostile-negative" style is treatable, but therapy must proceed with caution, and the therapist must be vigilant to ensure the protection of all family members. We typically do not provide family therapy for the "violent rape" families.

Family structure may be assessed in a variety of ways. We find Olson's Family Inventories[2] particularly the Family Adaptability and Cohesion Scales (FACES) extremely useful in providing a composite family structure and a comparison with "normal" families. Particularly useful are the comparison scores among family members, which provides a view of the family from each member's perspective. Family structure is also assessed through family role-playing, family sculpture or family drawings, seating arrangements, and through observing the flow of communication (i.e., who talks to or through whom and when). Finally, direct questions are addressed to the entire family regarding privacy, outside friends, the ability of family members to separate and do things on their own, the flexibility of family rules, and power.

Socio-Environmental Factors

A variety of socio-environmental dimensions have been hypothesized as contributing to the expression of intrafamily sexual abuse, and thus to a family's vulnerability. These factors include those environmental or community conditions that are continually present for a family, and include chronic stress (Justice and Justice, 1979; Renshaw, 1982); social isolation; and opportunity factors (Finkelhor, 1978). Also important is the tolerance toward incestuous behavior of the community in which the family lives. And finally, of overriding importance is the general cultural acceptance of male supremacy that has in a variety of ways tolerated, or even encouraged abuse of women and children (Herman and Hirschman, 1977). Although the latter factor is present for all families, the degree to which a family accepts traditional male-female roles may make the family more vulnerable to intrafamily sexual abuse.

It is essential that the family's immediate environment be assessed both for the direct impact it has on the family and the attitudes about its environment the family has. Besides direct questioning of the family regarding stress, social isolation, and attitudes regarding male-female roles, we have found the Family Inventory of Life Events and Changes (Olson et al., 1982) quite useful in providing information on the stress levels and major life changes impacting the family. A working knowledge of the community in which the family lives will be important in assessing the degree of tolerance to incest found there. Most important, constant awareness on the part of the therapist that a family is a part of a larger context that permits and supports the abusive interactions is essential throughout the course of therapy.

It should be again noted that, according to our vulnerability framework, even if a family were vulnerable to intrafamily sexual abuse, i.e., they have a greater number of the above vulnerability factors present, it does not mean that incest will automatically occur. The family must also have a precipitating event present, and have few coping mechanisms available, or there will still be a lower likelihood of its expression.

PRECIPITATING EVENTS

A number of precipitating conditions or events have been described as typically preceding an incestuous episode. The most commonly cited are substance abuse, particularly alcohol intoxication (Maisch, 1973;

Virkkunen, 1974); mother's absence from home (Batten, 1983), or a major acute stress (Justice and Justice, 1979).

Information regarding the precipitant conditions or events is usually obtained during the intake process. From our experience, many families will state alcohol use or abuse as their theoretical causal hypothesis. It is very common to hear "I was drunk at the time; that's the reason I did such a thing." We have found that alcohol use is never the *cause* but instead a precipitant; that is, a family that is *not* vulnerable to incest will never engage in incestuous behavior, no matter how drunk the perpetrator becomes.

FAMILY COPING MECHANISMS

Many highly vulnerable families with precipitating factors leading to the expression of incest never engage in incestuous behavior. This is because there are coping mechanisms available to a family, such as a strong social network, consistent religious beliefs, or the availability of a local support group such as Parent's Anonymous or Parent's United (Giaretto, 1978). In fact, we view having been in therapy as a coping mechanism in and of itself in that they will now have the option to discuss problems and feelings, including sexual, with the therapist at a later date.

Family strengths can be assessed in a variety of ways, including direct questioning of the family during interviews. We have found the Family Strengths and Family Coping Strategies Inventories (Olson et al., 1982), however, particularly useful in providing an objective measurement of important dimensions, such as problem solving abilities, the availability of extended family, the ability to recognize and utilize social networks, and the degree of religious beliefs.

ASSESSMENT PROCEDURES

Our assumption is that intrafamily sexuality will express itself only in families that are; (1) highly vulnerable based on the family of origin of the parents, personality characteristics of the individual family members, family dynamics, and environmental conditions; (2) have had a precipitating event occur; and (3) lack sufficient coping mechanisms that would prevent its expression. The goal of the clinical assessment is to obtain information as to which factors are present which made the family particularly vulnerable, what precipitants were or typically are involved, and where the family's coping mechanisms are lacking. Once this information is gathered, a treatment plan whose goals are to reduce vulnerability, decrease possible precipitators, and increase family coping skills can be designed.

To accomplish this, we have found that a formal assessment procedure taking a minimum of four weeks is necessary, and includes individual, family, and collateral (with extended family members and outside systems, such as school personnel, etc.) assessment sessions when possible. We try and include the entire family in the assessment process and to have at least two full family sessions during this phase of our program. However, family diagnostic sessions will take place only when we feel confident that the child and any other family member is completely safe from the possibility of further abuse.

The actual configuration of the sessions, such as which members of the family will be present, is dependent upon the emotional and physical availability of the various family members. After meeting with different family members and describing our program, we usually arrange for the father, mother, and daughter to undergo psychological evaluations to assess individual vulnerability factors, and to determine the need for immediate intervention or hospitalization. The therapist over time sees family members individually, different dyadic relationships, and the family as a whole. By viewing the family in its component and whole parts, the therapist may fully evaluate the individuals and family with regard to type, structure, and communication.

Many families resist including the non-abused children in the assessment sessions. Often they were not told about the incest, and the parents are afraid of the possible reactions the children may have. We usually insist that these children are included in the sessions, although we assure the parents that we (the therapists) will not be the ones to disclose the details, that this is the responsibility of the parents. (We do require an eventual disclosure to the entire family during our "Apology Session;" see pp. 89). What is discussed is how the family is handling the crisis they are in, how the family is adjusting to the father (or daughter) being gone from the home, and what the family wants to happen as a result of therapy. The content of the sessions is less important than facilitating a process by which the therapist may assess the family process.

Development of Treatment Plans

The treatment plan should be developed to reduce a family's vulnerability to incest, decrease the occurrence of the precipitants, and increase the family coping mechanisms. Techniques to reduce vulnerability should focus on those dimensions which contribute most to vulnerability and are most accessible. In our experience, the most accessible dimensions are family system factors, individual personality or psychopathology factors, and coping mechanisms, in that order. Although the remaining dimensions may be quite important in the contribution to a family's vulnerability to intrafamily sexual abuse, they may be difficult or impossible to intervene upon.

SUMMARY

A framework for the clinical assessment of intrafamily sexual abuse was presented to allow clinicians to evaluate the multiple dimensions involved with the expression of incestuous behavior. It was hypothesized that in most cases, there is no one cause of intrafamily sexual abuse. Instead, all families are endowed with a degree of vulnerability based on individual, family, and environmental factors, which express as incest if a precipitating event takes place, and the family has few coping mechanisms available to them. It was suggested that a family be formally assessed along these dimensions using a variety of evaluation techniques, including individual and family clinical interviews, objective and projective assessment devices, and ongoing clinical observation. Treatment plans should then be developed to focus intervention on reducing those factors contributing most to the family's vulnerability, decreasing the likelihood of the precipitating events repeating, and to increase the family's coping mechanisms.

NOTES

1. Available from the first author upon request.
2. Available from David H. Olson, Family Social Science, 290 McNeal Ave., University of Minnesota, St. Paul, MN 55108.

REFERENCES

Batten, D. A. (1983). Incest: A review of the literature. *Medical and Scientific Law*, 23, 245–253.
Conte, J. (1982). Sexual abuse of children: Enduring questions for social work. In Jon R. Conte and David A. Shore (Eds.), *Social work and child sexual abuse*, New York: Haworth Press.
Finkelhor, D. (1978). Psychological, cultural, and structural factors in incest and family sexual abuse. *Journal of Marriage and Family Counseling*, 4, 45–50.
Garbriano, J. (1977). The human ecology of child maltreatment. *Journal of Marriage and the Family*, 39, 721–735.
Giaretto, H. (1978). Humanistic treatment of father-daughter incest. *Journal of Humanistic Psychology*, 18.
Gottschalk, L. A. (1983). Vulnerability to "stress." *American Journal of Psychotherapy*, 37, 5–23.
Herman, J., and Hirschman, L. (1977). Father-daughter incest. *Signs*, 4, 735–756.
Herman, J., and Hirschman, L. (1981). Families at risk for father-daughter incest. *American Journal of Psychiatry*, 138, 967–970.
Justice, B., and Justice, R. (1979). *The broken taboo: Sex in the family*. New York: Human Sciences Press.

Larson, N., and Maddox, J. Incest management and treatment: Family systems vs. victim advocacy approaches. Paper presented at the Annual Meeting of the American Association for Marriage and Family Therapy, San Francisco, October, 1984.

Maisch, H. (1973). *Incest*. London: Andre Deutsch.

Meiselman, K. C. (1978). *Incest*. San Francisco: Jossey-Bass.

Olson D. H., et al. (1982). *Family Inventories*. St. Paul, MN: Family Social Science, University of Minnesota.

Renshaw, D. (1982). *Incest: Understanding and treatment*. Boston: Little, Brown.

Rosenthal, D. (1971). *Genetics of psychopathology*. New York: McGraw Hill.

Rosenfeld, A. (1979). Endogamic incest and the victim-perpetrator model. *American Journal of Diseases of Children*, 133, 406–410.

Straus, M. A. (1980). Stress and child abuse. In C. Henry Kempe and Ray E. Helfer (Eds.), *The Battered Child* (3rd Ed), Chicago: University of Chicago Press.

Summit, R., and Kryso, J. (1978). Sexual abuse of children: A clinical spectrum. *American Journal of Orthopsychiatry*, 48, 237–251.

Tierney, K. J., and Corwin, D. L. (1983). Exploring intrafamilial child sexual abuse: A systems approach. In David Finkelhor et al., (Eds.), *The dark side of families*. Beverly Hills: Sage.

Virkkunen, M. (1974). Incest offenses and alcoholism. *Medical and Scientific Law*, 14, 124.

Will, D. (1983). Approaching the incestuous and sexually abusive family. *Journal of Adolescence*, 6, 229–246.

Zubin, J., and Spring, B. (1977). Vulnerability: A new view of schizophrenia. *Journal of Abnormal Psychology*, 86, 103–126.

Structural and Functional Variables in Incest Family Systems: Implications for Assessment and Treatment

Noel R. Larson
James W. Maddock

INTRODUCTION

The phenomenal growth of incest treatment programs in recent years has made it apparent that professionals working with family sexual abuse may have very different underlying assumptions about the nature of the problem. These differences appear most dramatically between professional groups, for example, between attorneys, child protection workers and psychotherapists. These variations promote a lack of coordination in the identification of sexual abuse and its aftermath; sometimes, the professionals involved even polarize into opposing "camps." Workers in child protective services and correctional institutions typically emphasize victim advocacy, external control of incestuous families and an individual approach to treatment. Therapists with a family orientation often argue that incest is best understood and treated from a systems perspective, that is, as a symptom of distorted elements in family process. However, even therapists who are concerned about the entire incest family differ in their theoretical orientations, have varying therapuetic skills, operate in diverse contexts and therefore develop treatment programs which are differentially effective with the incest family population.

Earlier efforts to conceptualize incestuous behavior (e.g., Weinberg, 1955; Stoller, 1975) focused on incest as a subcategory of pedophilia, using dynamic models of individual psychopathology. More recently, researchers (e.g., Justice and Justice, 1976; Thorman, 1983) have described incest behavior in terms of interaction factors in the family context. The stance taken in this chapter is an integration of these views, i.e., that incest is a distortion of the sexual dimension of family experience, arising out of a complex combination of mutually influencing

The authors are both Licensed Consulting Psychologists at Meta Resources Psychotherapy and Training Institute in St. Paul, MN, and adjunct faculty members at the University of Minnesota.

variables in each of four "existential" categories: intrapsychic, systemic, developmental and situational (Maddock, 1983). The remainder of this chapter will focus primarily on systemic variables, examining certain structural and functional factors that can aid in understanding the incest phenomenon and are suggestive of certain steps to be taken in the assessment and treatment processes.

STRUCTURAL ANALYSIS OF INCESTUOUS BEHAVIOR

Previously, Larson (1980) has proposed that incest be understood as a reflection of "boundary disturbances" in four areas: (1) the boundary between the family and its social environment; (2) the boundary between adult and child generations in the family; (3) interpersonal/role boundaries between family members; and (4) intrapsychic boundaries within family members (pp. 71–72). A "boundary" delineates the organizational wholeness, or "autonomy," of a given system (Keeney, 1983). The more autonomous a system is, the more organizationally "closed" it is. In addition, the system's boundary is the key variable in determining the overall structure of the system, which in turn is the most powerful factor influencing what goes on inside the system (i.e., within its boundaries), as well as between the system and its environment (Dell, 1985). Ultimately, then, a boundary is the key factor in determining what a given system *is*, how it is organized, what processes will occur inside it, how it will interact with its environment—and even in predicting how the system is likely to behave in the future. In the view taken here, incest is a reflection of a family system that is relatively closed, undifferentiated and rigid in both structure and function, i.e., a product of substantial boundary disturbances.

Family/Society Boundary

In a variety of ways, incest families protect their sexual secret by constructing barriers between the family system and its social environment. Insulating themselves from critical social feedback that could serve to influence their behavior, family members can draw *only* upon each other for emotional support, self-esteem maintenance and reality-testing. An implicit rule evolves that *all* important emotional needs are to be met within the family system. Others to whom family members might turn for sharing and intimacy are regarded as hostile intruders who in some way threaten the survival of the family unit. This closed, highly autonomous family system limits opportunities for growth and renewal, producing a certain "scarcity of resources" while fostering inappropriate overdependence among family members and producing "enmeshment," i.e., limitations on self-differentiation (Minuchin, 1974).

When these families come into contact with outside social and/or legal systems, their boundaries rigidify even more as they attempt to maintain homeostasis and keep the family intact. The harder that therapists or others try to penetrate this protective shell, the more the family as a whole resists any kind of change and may take on the veneer of a "united front." Indirect approaches to investigation and treatment rather than heavy confrontation appear to be the most successful means of promoting positive change. At the same time, systems outside the incest family must appear powerful enough for family members to respect, since concentrations of power reflect a structural fit between the family and its environment. Simply put, power (even abusive power) is a language that the incest family understands.

Intergenerational Boundary

The dependency problems and enmeshment produced by the emotional isolation of incest family members promotes the blurring of boundaries between adult and child generations. Family members are pressed into service to meet each other's needs regardless of age or developmental stage. While some literature on incest (e.g., Thorman, 1983) has identified a reversal of roles between mother and daughter, we believe that the phenomenon can more accurately be described as "role-confusion" and "role-exchange" among *all* incest family members. Contrary to the functioning of healthy families, children in incest families perform developmental tasks appropriate to adults, and parents abdicate certain important responsibilities in order to compete with their children for limited emotional resources. Thus the nurturance necessary to healthy development (Erickson, 1963) may not be available to children, creating deficits in important areas of psychosocial development and exposing them prematurely to adult tasks—including the incestuous contact. This dilemma is further complicated by the tendency of these "parentified" children to respond with pseudo-mature behavior that is adaptive in the short-run, while promoting in the long-run a grandiose belief that they are capable of meeting any and all emotional needs of other people, even at their own expense. Thus the incest victims of one generation set the stage for later selecting spouses who will again victimize them—and very likely also their children.

Interpersonal Boundaries

Since human beings are open organismic systems in themselves, it is also possible to speak of "interpersonal boundaries" in a family. These are *demarcations of psychosocial influence and meaning* which extend beyond the skin of the individual into the interpersonal environment (Kantor and Lehr, 1975). Incest families are often characterized by substantial "boundary diffusion" between members (Bowen, 1978), i.e., lacking autonomy and the power of self-differentiation. In order to be supported and nurtured in a system characterized by enmeshment and scarce resources, members must yield their autonomy in order to belong. Personal boundaries become diffuse; interaction produces symbiotic relationship patterns in which each member feels that his/her survival is dependent upon the emotional and psychosocial status of the other members. This goes beyond—though also includes—the symbiotic bond often noted between incest perpetrator and victim; it permeates the family and is more accurately conveyed in Bowen's concept of "undifferentiated family ego mass" (Kerr, 1981). Differentiation of self, involving independent thought, feeling, desire and behavior by family members, is threatening to the structure of the incest family system. Differentness is experienced as distance, and individuality is viewed as alienation and disloyalty. Control becomes a critical factor in family structure, and members who threaten the system through autonomous behavior can become the targets of scapegoating and escalating abuse.

These variables trigger a variety of dysfunctional interaction patterns within the family, including: (1) a pervasive fear of abandonment, along with compensatory defense mechanisms to avoid such an outcome; (2) an increased atmosphere of shame and low self-esteem among family members; (3) a variety of "double-bind" interaction patterns that foster schizoid behavior and preclude escape (Watzlawick et al., 1967); and (4) a range of "instrumental" behaviors—particularly sex-related—that evolve as a means of coping with stress (Straus, 1980). These dysfunctional patterns become rigidly structured into the behavior of family members, producing a family lifestyle directed at overcoming a pervasive sense of intrapersonal and interpersonal emptiness.

Intrapsychic Boundaries

The term "boundary" has been a useful metaphor for analyzing individual psychodynamics since the time of Freud (Freud, 1938). Intrapsychic boundaries reflect the "parts" of personality structure, whose significance is in their relationship to each other and to the whole psychic apparatus. In the healthy individual, the various psychic structures are integrated in such a way as to support the autonomy and wholeness of the personality system and to function in a coherent, coordinated way (Slipp, 1984). When so-called "psychopathology" occurs, the psyche can be said to be structured in a maladaptive way, i.e., a way that does not fit well with the requirements of the environment, with resulting distortions in meaning and in behavior.

To minimize the cognitive dissonance and emotional pain created by the intrafamilial abuse while maintaining the emotional dependency and interpersonal enmeshment, incest family members rely heavily on defense mechanisms. Often the most powerful defense is *denial*, the inability to consciously recognize certain feelings and/or experiences. Denial is common in abusing families of all kinds. It is adaptive in coping with pain and trauma, and it helps to minimize the threat of exposure to the world outside the family. Denial does not focus only on the incest; it is pervasive throughout each individual's own experience and throughout the family. It enables family members to engage in exquisitely distorted thought patterns which lead, in turn, to intricate rationalizations of symptomatic and/or problematic behaviors.

Despite their usefulness at one level, denial and related defense mechanisms, used consistently over time, impair feedback processes within the family and distort members' perceptions of outside reality. Thinking that they *must* continue certain behaviors to survive, family members remain stuck in their destructive victim/victimizer patterns, thereby increasing their feelings of shame and powerlessness, which in turn promote further emotional isolation and perceptual distortion. Due to the protective nature of denial, family members are usually thrown into crisis when the incest secret is revealed to the outside world and/or is made available to be dealt with openly within the family. Frequently the crisis causes further denial as the family coalesces to resist change. Emotional regression is common at this time, and accounts of the incest are likely to shift relative to the amount of resistance perceived as necessary to individual and collective survival.

Taken together, these four boundary disturbances in the incest family reveal a skewed, or distorted, family structure in which sex is a reflection of "dis-ease" and a vehicle for abusive, exploitive interaction. Structurally speaking, the sexuality of the abusive family is typically characterized by some or all of the following (Maddock, 1983):

1. Lack of respect for one or both genders, and for the role-related behaviors of one or both genders; rigidity in the role-expectations of both genders.
2. Poor body/self image, and a general shame-based, negative view of sex and the body.
3. Distortion of the erotic potential of individual family members, including insensitivity to the needs of children at various stages of psychosexual development; inconsistency in approaches to sexual behavior, restraining it unnecessarily on one arena (e.g., dating) while fostering it inappropriately in another (e.g., oral sex with parent).
4. Exploitation of the touch and body-contact needs of members, ignoring developmental readiness.

5. Lack of respect for personal privacy, both physical and emotional.
6. Lack of an effective communication system regarding sex, including misinformation, paucity of feelings expressed, and attitude distortion.
7. Lack of balance in power, control and influence between partners in the marital dyad.
8. Lack of a satisfactory and mutually meaningful erotic relationship in the marital dyad, including loss of expressiveness, reduced affection exchange and little capacity for negotiation of sexual interest.
9. Lack of an appropriate parental role structure through which to guide, protect and nurture the unfolding of children's sexuality in age-appropriate ways.
10. Lack of knowledge about sex; rather, an emphasis on stereotypes, myths and distortions.
11. Lack of an overall sexual value system to transmit from one generation to the next; inability to support autonomous decisionmaking by family members.
12. Overly rigid social boundaries which prevent appropriate information exchange with, and consensual validation by, the family's social environment regarding sex-related beliefs, attitudes and values.

A FUNCTIONAL TYPOLOGY OF INCEST FAMILIES

The motivations of incest perpetrators have been explored, and varied findings have been reported (Groth et al., 1982; Langevin, 1983). Similarly, family theoreticians have speculated on the function of incest in the family system, some reporting that it seems to be a way for certain families to stay together, others that it may be an attempt on the part of someone in the family to break free from the enmeshed structure (Justice and Justice, 1976; Sholevar, 1975). In the view taken here, incest does not serve the same functions in every family in which it occurs, and its motivations and purposes may remain obscure. However, like all human behavior, incest is *meaningful* within the context in which it occurs. Its meaning evolves from the particular patterns of interaction that characterize a given family; then, the meaning of the behavior shared by family members serves as the basis for further sequences of behavior, which in turn lead to new meanings, and so on (Barton and Alexander, 1981). Understanding the meaning of behavior in terms of its context does not imply linear causality. Rather, it demonstrates how behavior can be created and maintained by a circular and reciprocal process of "meaning-making'' that is central to shared family experience. Of course, the forms that actions can take in a given family are limited by its structure, and we have already noted that the structure of the incest family permits—even encourages—the sexual abuse. But the *function* that the incest serves in a given family system arises out of the network of meanings which ties together family members and influences their patterns of interaction.

In incest families, the sexual involvement with children can be categorized as serving one of four basic functions in interpersonal exchange processes: affectional process, erotic process, aggression process or the process of expressing rage. When placed on a continuum and integrated with other functional variables (Table I), a typology is created which is useful for assessment and treatment planning for incest families.

Affection-Exchange Process

A significant amount of incestuous behavior appears to serve as a means of affection-exchange between two or more family members of different generations. Many incest fathers engage in a quasi-courtship process with their daughters in a misguided attempt to show affection and feel emotionally close. This objective can increase the likelihood that actual sexual intercourse will take place between father and daughter as a consummation of the relationship between them as "lovers."

Important to the development of this type of incest behavior is the significant lack of healthier, more normal forms of physical nurturing and affection available to family members. This increases the likelihood that the child will accept—and perhaps even seek out—sexual contact in an attempt to meet natural needs for touch, physical closeness, affection and emotional support. Physical force and other forms of coercion are largely unnecessary in the affectionally-based incest family, since the child may appear cooperative and compliant. Consistent with the theme of a parent-child "love affair," the sexual activity is usually conducted in a highly clandestine manner, and elaborate steps may be taken to deceive other family members (who, like the spouses in many extramarital affairs, may nevertheless "know" that they are part of a triangle).

The incest victim herself may be considerably reluctant to expose the sexual secret and thereby be forced to give up her privileged status with her father. She may develop a hostile, competitive relationship with her mother and her siblings and/or align with her father in intrafamilial conflicts. Unless unwittingly revealed by the participants or accidentally discovered by others, this type of incest may continue until one of several developmental factors intervenes to produce significant conflict between parent and child; for example, the daughter becoming interested in a

Table I

Incest Family Typology

AFFECTION EXCHANGE PROCESS	EROTIC EXCHANGE PROCESS	AGGRESSION EXCHANGE PROCESS	EXPRESSION OF RAGE PROCESS
Positive Intent	Positive Intent	Negative Intent	Negative Intent
Object Connection	Object Connection	No Object Connection	Object Displacement
Non-violent	Non-violent	Often Violent	Violent, Life-Threatening
Power Motive Minimal	Power Motive May Be Present	Power Motive Present	Power Motive Primary
Individual Psychopathology Not Critical	Individual Psychopathology Not Critical	Individual Psychopathology May Be Critical	Individual Psychopathology Critical and Primary

dating relationship with a boyfriend or the father turning his attention to a younger sibling.

Interviewing and testing members of an affectionally-based incest family may reveal some anxiety, depression and stronger-than-average dependency needs. However, individual psychopathology usually is not sufficient to inhibit relatively effective functioning in most areas of life. This is particularly true for the perpetrator. The child may eventually begin to suffer some stress-related symptoms and/or social maladjustment based upon isolation from peers and conflict with other family members.

Erotic-Exchange Process

The incest family that eroticizes relationships among its members can be labeled "pansexual." Sexual meaning is attached to everyday inter-action patterns among family members, often including the extended kinship network as well. The incestuous behavior in these families may involve both parents and most or all the children and may have a game-like quality. The family appears to be bonded largely through its projections of eroticism into language, physical appearance, clothes, recreation and humor. Lack of privacy is equated with trust; family members may be shamed and/or guilted by others when they try to exercise control over who has access to their bodies, their behavior in bathroom or bedroom, their personal spaces or possessions. Family photograph albums or home movies may include sexual depictions, extending even into the making of child pornography for commercial sale. Sexual variations are quite common, including voyeurism, exhibitionism, group sex among family members (and perhaps members of other, similarly-inclined families) and the encouragement of family members to use sex as a medium of exchange with their social environment as well (e.g., prostitution). Unlike the other types of incest families, the pansexual family often allows significant individuals to enter its erotic sphere: the hired farm hand, a favorite in-law, the live-in babysitter, the trusted friend.

In erotically-based incest families, the sexual contact may or may not include sexual intercourse, since much of the focus is on teasing and titillation which does not require consummation to have meaning and reinforcement value. Violence is relatively seldom used to insure compliance, since family members are socialized into a pervasive erotic ambiance. However, power and control exist as issues just under the surface, and thus there can be strong but subtle influences which make participation by individual members difficult to resist.

Pansexual families may be able to maintain the secret sexual behavior for a long time, particularly because the incestuous pattern does not fit traditional criminal definitions or the public's stereotype of sexual abuse (this has begun to change as a result of several widely-publicized cases in recent years). When the incest behavior does surface, there is often lack of persuasive evidence and/or lack of cooperation by family members who understandably fear the consequences of exposure. The problem may come to light in a variety of ways: inappropriate sexual behavior by younger family members at school, noticeable sexual acting-out in the community, extra-familial sexual abuse by one of the family members, even the tracing of neighborhood "stories" about the family.

As in the affectionally-based incest family, individual psychopathology is relatively rare among pansexual family members. However, there may be sub-clinical levels of a cluster of factors typically designated as "characterological," or societal-variant. Often the integration of eroticism into family interaction patterns is so complete—and denial so well-established—that family members have stopped noticing the sexual meanings and have lost all traces of anxiety related to their socially atypical behavior. However, it is not uncommon for the family structure to include one or members (particularly children) who are symptomatic: suicidal, anorectic, self-mutilating, even overtly psychotic.

Aggression-Exchange Process

Unable to express hostility in more appropriate ways, aggression-based incest families use sexualized anger to deal with their frustration and disappointment over various aspects of their lives. In these families, the perpetrator may deal angrily—even violently—with the victim, who may be only a scapegoat for the perpetrator's masked hostility toward another family member. Thus, for example, father/daughter incestuous contact may occur in connection with the perpetrator's wish to punish his wife for her lack of attention and affection. Or an adolescent male may sexually exploit his younger sister in retaliation for what he perceives as abandonment or rejection by his father, whom he believes shows intense favoritism toward the girls in the family (which may itself have an incestuous element).

Although free-floating hostility is prevalent in this type of incest family, members typically feel powerless to have any kind of direct impact upon each other. Yet because he is part of a system characterized by diffuse interpersonal boundaries, the perpetrator is often convinced that his victimizing actions will negatively affect the person toward whom his hostility is actually directed. However, in a self-protective maneuver he usually chooses the most vulnerable member of the family as his victim, and thus his real intentions and motives do not become known. The resulting lack of direct feedback from the real source of his hostility only serves to deepen his feelings of powerlessness and helps to maintain the family rule that direct confrontation and negotiation between conflicting members cannot occur.

The intent to hurt someone via incestuous activity contrasts with the dynamics of the affectionally-based and erotically-based incest families, in which the behavior serves as a misguided effort at positive communication. This aggression-based incest dynamic creates an atmosphere that fosters individual psychopathology as well as the distortions in family structure. Suicidal depression and various forms of self-destructive behavior often result, based upon the underlying lack of impulse control coupled with the fear of direct interpersonal conflict.

Rage Expression Process

The final functional category of incestuous behavior is rooted in the intra-individual system, i.e., psychopathology. Here the perpetrator acts out his/her existential *rage* upon a family member who is least threatening and resistant, typically a younger child. This is not focused anger, but a primitive expression of high-energy affect resulting from longstanding frustration. Typically the perpetrator's rage is rooted in his/her own long history as a victim of neglect or abuse, creating an internal psychic structure characterized by continuous threats to survival. Less often, but not infrequently, the rageful incest perpetrator is fueled by full-blown psychotic processes. The result is that some perpetrators present themselves directly with enraged affect. Others seem oddly detached from any affect, but demonstrate little or no control of abusive or violent behavior, conducted in a cold and calculating way accompanied by earnest rationalizations. Sometimes these patterns are bizarre, as in the case of the father who physically beat and anally raped his young adolescent son in order to teach him, the father explained, "what he has to watch out for from those damn faggots." Life-threatening violence can accompany sexual abuse in the rage-based incest family.

If the incestuous activity in the rage-based family is sudden and violent, other family members—or the victim—may respond by reporting the event so that outsiders can intervene. Here, fear overrides family loyalties. If the abuse is episodic, family members are more likely to "learn to live with it," although defensive measures may be taken by at least some individuals; for example, children staying overnight at the houses of friends. Sometimes, however, the rage of the perpetrator—and perhaps other family members—serves as an organizing principle for the family, and the system structures itself around the rage as a source of power. Even the defensive measures taken may become part of the family's social script. Some family members may learn how to take a generalized "victim" stance toward life; others may pride themselves on learning how to "con" the perpetrator in order to avoid victimization, a maneuver that is generalized to others outside of the family.

All in all, the rage-based incest family is one of the most pathological of family systems and is among the most likely to contribute to the individual psychopathology of its members. The functional adaptations that permit survival in such a family are often at odds with the requirements of effective interpersonal relationships and healthy behavior patterns in the outside world.

CONSIDERATIONS IN ASSESSMENT AND TREATMENT

At least until recent years, there has been little consensus on programmatic treatment approaches to incest families (Bulkley, 1981; Carnes, 1983; Knopp, 1984; Kroth, 1979; MacFarlane and Bulkley, 1982; Renshaw, 1982). Even today, there are few "pure" programs based upon a single theoretical approach; however, underlying conceptual frameworks are usually discernible in a given program. Long-term outcome studies are not yet available, though most programs report that perpetrators and/or incest families are "helped" by involvement in therapy. Recidivism is the outcome most often cited in attempting to objectively assess the success of a particular approach to treatment.

If the premise of the typology presented here is true; namely, that incestuous behavior serves different functions in different families, then it would appear to be important to assess the *meaning and function* of the incest in a given family when planning for its treatment. Too often, we believe, a family is treated in a certain way because of the particular characteristics of a treatment program that exists in its geographic vicinity rather than on the basis of the kind of approach which would be predicted to be most effective given the specific characteristics of the family. For example, a highly confrontive program that focuses on identifying and exchanging anger between family members may be very useful to an aggression-based incest family, while the same treatment approach to an affection-based family may generate confusion, shame, anxiety and resistance since it will very likely fail to address *this family's experience* in a meaningful way. On this basis, any given treatment program will be randomly successful with a reasonable number of client families. Informal discussion by workers in the field suggests that families who drop out of treatment programs because they do not seem to "fit" (assuming coercive legal measures are lacking or have been concluded) are high risks for recidivism.

The four categories described above can serve as guidelines for developing treatment approaches that are highly "coupled" (Maturana, 1985) with both the functional meanings and the structural characteristics of various incest families (Table II). The remainder of this chapter will briefly describe some implications for treatment of the four kinds of incest families.

Table II

Incest Family Typology Treatment Considerations

AFFECTION EXCHANGE PROCESS	EROTIC EXCHANGE PROCESS	AGGRESSION EXCHANGE PROCESS	EXPRESSION OF RAGE PROCESS
Outpatient Treatment	Outpatient Treatment	Outpatient/Inpatient Trtmt.	Inpatient Treatment
Family Therapy Primary	Group Therapy for Family Members Primary	Group Therapy for Family Members Primary	Individual Therapy Primary
Separation Not Necessary	Separation Sometimes Necessary	Separation Usually Necessary	Separation Necessary And Critical
Perhaps Group Therapy	Family Therapy	Family Therapy	Group Therapy
	Marital Therapy	Marital Therapy	Perhaps Family Therapy
		Perhaps Individual Therapy	Perhaps Marital Therapy
Structural/Strategic Family Approaches, Supportive Group Therapy	Confrontive, "Addiction" Group Approaches, and Structural/Strategic Family and Marital Therapy	Confrontive Group Approaches, Structural/Stragetic Family and Marital Therapy, Empathic Individual Therapy	Empathic, psychodynamic Individual Therapy, Supportive Group Therapy, Structural/Strategic Marital and Family Therapy

Treatment for Affection-Based Incest Families

The family for whom incest is an affectional-exchange process has a number of strengths upon which to capitalize during treatment. Its underlying theme is the desire for positive contact, and the perpetrator seldom uses violence or coercion. Family members need to be encouraged to function as individuals, but in a coordinated manner with each other in order to meet needs and accomplish tasks in a mutually beneficial way. Boundary issues can usually be worked on rather explicitly. The disruption of bringing the incest out into the open often provides sufficient motivation to forestall recurrences. Therefore outpatient treatment, with an emphasis on the entire family, is typically most effective and efficient. The family often has other resources and strengths that can be utilized in treatment, including affiliative needs that can be directed at forming supportive networks with others *outside* the family—thus helping to break down the artificial rigidity of the boundary between the family and its social environment. With a focus on self-differentiation within the family system, techniques common to structural and strategic family therapy approaches appear to be effective with this type of family. Usually, it is most helpful if the perpetrator can remain in the home with other family members for the duration of the treatment process. Individual therapy or participation in a group can be useful to some perpetrators, where the focus is on increased self-esteem and personal identity issues.

Treatment for Erotic-Based Incest Families

Because misguided eroticism has permeated nearly all aspects of life in the pansexual family, a more directive approach to treatment is typically helpful. However, because the underlying motivations are still positive (in most cases), outpatient treatment programs can be effective. Living arrangements for family members should be dealt with carefully and thoroughly. Erotic interaction patterns are so well-established that they are often difficult to reorganize, and physical separation of some combination of family members may be called for. Open group homes, halfway-house type residences and other living arrangements that de-emphasize sex as a basis for social interaction can be useful adjuncts to treatment of various family members.

The combination of rigid sexual stereotypes and role-related power struggles that so often characterize pansexual families makes education, attitude change and reality testing high priorities for promoting change in the family system. Thus group therapy with peers is useful, particularly in the earlier stages of treatment. Perpetrators' and victims' groups, peer support programs such as Parents United, sexual addiction treatment models—any may be helpful in facilitating alternative ways of experiencing the role of sexuality in interpersonal relationships. Marital therapy with a sexual focus is likely to be very useful for the perpetrator and his spouse. And integrative family therapy can be added in later stages of treatment when intrapersonal and interpersonal boundary issues have been sufficiently resolved to permit the development of intimacy and nurturance in positive ways between family members.

Treatment for Aggression-Based Incest Families

Depending upon the assessed degree of impulse control and the propensity of unresolved power struggles to lead to further coercive sexual exploitation or even to violence, members of aggression-based incest families may require highly-controlled living situations. Perpetrators can benefit from inpatient treatment, and victims from the protection of a sheltered residence or foster care home. It is common for family members to be separated from each other during at least the early and middle phases of treatment; however, some treatment programs maintain this separation far past the time when it is necessary and/or useful.

Highly confrontive group treatment approaches can facilitate family members learning to deal creatively with anger and conflict in relationships, without linking these to sex. Marital therapy with an emphasis on conflict management and resolution is usually necessary. Similarly, family therapy focusing on intergenerational power struggles and developmental issues can serve to open up channels for negotiation and problem-solving. All aspects of treatment for family members should attend to the underlying issues of shame and low self-esteem. Some members may require a period of intense individual therapy to help them repair self-deficits and build sufficient ego strength to be able to maintain an identity in the context of close interpersonal relationships.

Toward the end of treatment, integrative family therapy is often indicated to rebuild the system toward a coherent *family* identity. Here, the focus is typically on trust, repair of previously-ruptured relationships, creative handling of conflict, forgiveness, and creating a plan for a common future. It should be noted that some anger-based incest families remain permanently split, their negative history simply too powerful to overcome, their vulnerability too great to permit trust.

Treatment for Rage-Based Incest Families

The propensity for violence and/or the effects of pathological behavior of family members should be the overriding factor in determining the structure and process of treating rage-based incest families. Closed inpatient treatment is typically necessary for the perpetrator, who is usually unable to control his/her episodes of sexual abuse. A combination of individual and group therapy is helpful to the perpetrator in uncovering and restructuring deep-seated emotional conflicts. Empathic, supportive group therapy is substantially more effective than high confrontation group styles, the latter tending to evoke shame—which is already deeply inter-twined with the rage that forms the core of the self. At some point in group or individual treatment, the perpetrator's own role as a victim typically surfaces, bringing with it waves of shame and anxiety that threaten to overwhelm the individual and, once again, render him impermeable to influence by those outside his own intrapsychic boundary. Until this therapeutic crisis has been successfully surmounted, the perpetrator is unlikely to be amenable to interactive therapy with other family members.

Various other members of the rage-based incest family may also require individual therapy to prepare them for more interactive, integrative treat-ment. Depending upon symptomatology and assessed degree of "dam-age," individuals may benefit from long-term therapy or even residential treatment. The issues of rage-based victimization are typically structured into the personality systems of most or all of these individuals if they have been part of a family system which has sustained the sexual abuse over a lengthy period of time (rather than simply discovering one or several episodes of abuse that result in the rapid removal of the perpetrator from the home). Many rage-based victims themselves manifest patterns of abuse perpetration, and soon the distinctions between perpetrator and victim become meaningless—other than for legal purposes.

Rage-based incest families often permanently dissolve, and the termi-nation of parental rights (sometimes voluntarily, sometimes involun-tarily) is not an uncommon sequel. Both parents may lack the interper-sonal capacity to provide support and nurturance for any or all of the children, and protection authorities are required to intervene. Even under these circumstances, however, integrative systems therapy is recom-mended to contribute to the healthy long-range functioning of the children, whose boundaries are once again threatened by the necessity of restructuring their model of a "family." Long-term foster parents and/or adoptive families can be included in treatment on an as-needed basis to assist in this restructuring process. Given the structural issues outlined earlier in this chapter, children raised in incest families are likely to enter surrogate families with inappropriate patterns of behavior—particularly in relation to the four boundary areas—that will necessitate extra efforts to integrate them into their new social environments.

CONCLUSION

This chapter has described certain structural and functional variables in the incest family system and drawn implications for assessment and treatment planning. It is the belief of the authors that a systemic understanding of the incest family allows for an integration of treatment modalities that includes both individually-focused and family-focused approaches without any inherent conflict. Further, this model enables the clinician or researcher to understand the structural determinants of incest in the family system (i.e., boundary disturbances), while recognizing that the *particular* meaning and function of the incestuous behavior in a given system must be taken into account in planning treatment or evaluating its effectiveness. Finally, it is hoped that the model can serve as a useful basis for identifying families at risk and evolving preventive methods in sexual health care.

REFERENCES

Barton, C. & Alexander, J.F. Functional Family Therapy. In A.S. Gurman & D. P. Kniskern (Eds.), *Handbook of Family Therapy*. New York: Brunner/Mazel, 1981.

Bowen, M. *Family Therapy in Clinical Practice*. New York: Jason Aronson, 1978.

Bulkley, J. *Innovations in the Prosecution of Child Sexual Abuse Cases*. National Legal Resource Center for Child Advocacy and Protection, American Bar Association. Washington D.C., 1981.

Carnes, P. *The Sexual Addiction*. Minneapolis: CompCare Publications, 1983.

Dell, P.F. Understanding Bateson and Maturana: Toward a Biological Foundations for the Social Sciences. *Journal of Marital and Family Therapy*, 1985, 11, 1–20.

Erikson, E. H. *Childhood and Society*. 2nd Ed. New York: W.W. Norton, 1963.

Freud, S. *The Basic Writings of Sigmund Freud*. Translated and Edited by A.A. Brill. New York: The Modern Library, 1938.

Groth, A.N., Hobson, W.F. & Gary, T.S. The Child Molester: Clinical Observations. In J.R. Conte & D.A. Shore (Eds.), *Social Work and Child Sexual Abuse*. New York: Haworth Press, 1982.

Justice, B. & Justice, R. *The Abusing Family*. New York: Human Sciences Press, 1976.

Kantor, D. & Lehr, W. *Inside the Family*. San Francisco: Jossey-Bass, 1977.

Keeney, B.P. *Aesthetics of Change*. New York: Guilford Press, 1983.

Kerr, M.E. Family Systems Theory and Therapy. In A.S. Gurman & D.P. Knishkern, *Handbook of Family Therapy*. New York: Brunner/Mazel, 1981.

Knopp, F.H. *Retraining Adult Sex Offenders: Methods and Models*. Syracuse, NY: Safer Society Press, 1984.

Kroth, J.A. *Child Sexual Abuse: Analysis of a Family Therapy Approach*. Springfield, IL: Charles C. Thomas, 1979.

Langevin, R. *Sexual Strands: Understanding and Treating Sexual Anomalies in Men*. Hillsdale, NJ: Lawrence Erlbaum Associates, 1983.

Larson, N.R. An Analysis of the Effectiveness of a State-Sponsored Program Designed to Teach Intervention Skills in the Treatment of Family Sexual Abuse. (Doctoral dissertation, University of Minnesota, 1980).

Maddock, J.W. Human Sexuality in the Life Cycle of the Family System. In J.D. Woody & R.H. Woody (Eds.), *Sexual Issues in Family Therapy*. Rockville, MD: Aspen Systems, 1983.

Maturana, H. A Biology of Cognition. Address presented at a Symposium on the Questions of Gregory Bateson. College of St. Benedict, St. Joseph, MN, May 6, 1985.

MacFarlane, K. & Bulkley, J. Treating Child Sexual Abuse: An Overview of Current Program Models. In J.R. Conte & D.A. Shore (Eds.), *Social Work and Child Sexual Abuse*. New York: Haworth Press, 1982.

Minuchin, S. *Families and Family Therapy*. Cambridge MA: Harvard University Press, 1974.

Renshaw, D.C. *Incest: Understanding and Treatment*. Boston: Little, Brown & Co., 1982.

Sholevar, G.P. A Family Therapist Looks at the Problem of Incest. *The Bulletin of the American Academy of Psychiatry and the Law*. 1975, 3 (1).

Slipp, S. *Object Relations: A Dynamic Bridge Between Individual and Family Treatment*. New York; Jason Aronson, 1984.

Stoller, R.J. *Perversion: The Erotic Form of Hatred*. New York: Pantheon Books, 1975.

Straus, M.A. Sexual Inequality and Wife Beating. In M.A. Straus & G.T. Hotaling (Eds.), *The Social Causes of Husband-Wife Violence*. Minneapolis: University of Minnesota Press, 1980.

Thorman, G. *Incestuous Families*. Springfield, IL: Charles C. Thomas, 1983.

Watzlawick, P., Beavin, J.H. & Jackson, D.D. *Pragmatics of Human Communication*. New York: W.W. Norton, 1967.

Weinberg, S.K. *Incest Behavior*. New York: Citadel Press, 1955.

The Contribution and Integration of Medicine in the Assessment and Treatment of Incest Victims

Howard B. Levy
Stephen H. Sheldon

The exact incidence of child sexual victimization is unknown. Reported estimates of occurrences vary from 1:4 adolescent females having experienced some form of sexual misuse before adulthood (Woodling et al., 1981) to 1:1,000 in the total adult female population having sustained sexual maltreatment (Cantwell, 1981). In 1982, approximately 23,000 case reports of child sexual abuse were submitted to the American Humane Association. These data as well as more recent information refute the myth that the sexual abuse of children is the result of acts perpetrated by strangers (Finkelhor, 1984). Ongoing studies poignantly validate data reflecting the vast number of perpetrators who are family members of the child. James, Womack, and Strauss reported in their study on child sexual abuse cases identified by family practitioners and pediatricians, that the majority of their cases were incestuous in nature (James et al., 1978).

The rapid increase in reported cases of incest is in part a response to the media's attention to the problem. However, legislative initiatives, improved diagnostic techniques, the initiation of discussions on the formerly taboo subject of incest, and an increasing awareness and involvement by various professional groups have all had a major impact on the number of identified cases. Nonetheless, in spite of better identification and disclosure procedures, less than half of the victims are identified and reported to physicians (Woodling et al., 1981). The medical community, although a gatekeeper in other areas, has continued to struggle in its attempts to identify a viable and practical role for itself. In an effort to delineate the potential contributions of the medical community in the assessment and

Howard B. Levy, MD, is Chairman of Pediatrics at Mount Sinai Hospital Medical Care Center; Chairman, Joint Program Pediatric Nephrology at Mount Sinai Hospital and Rush-Presbyterian-St. Luke's Medical Center; and Associate Professor at Rush Medical College, Chicago, Illinois.

Stephen H. Sheldon, DO, is Director of Educational Research and Development, Department of Pediatric at Mount Sinai Hospital; and Assistant Professor of Pediatrics and Preventive Medicine at Rush Medical College, Chicago, Illinois.

45

treatment of incest cases, the authors have selected a format which utilizes a simulated patient. This case presentation method exemplifies one of the several modalities of medical education used in our setting. It represents a sample portion from the training curriculum to train health care providers which the authors have developed in partnership with the Illinois Department of Children and Family Services. The curriculum consists of patient simulations, videotaped material of didactic and case presentation teaching methods, protocols, decision-making algorithms, as well as innovative interviewing techniques and tools. This specific patient simulation prototypes a generic method of "management" of sexually abused children by a physician as he or she attempts to work within the community of responses. In conjunction with other aspects of the training curriculum, this method allows for an active method of teaching health care providers to recognize and appropriately manage incest cases. It also encourages an active participation and dialogue with the multiple community systems comprising the response network in child incest cases.

THE CASE

Vicky Burrows was an unusually quiet, seemingly withdrawn four year old white female, who was brought to her doctor's office by her father. Mr. Burrows requested that Vicky be examined and treated for injuries which he alleged were inflicted one week previously by her 16 year old cousin, George. Mr. Burrows related that Goerge forced Vicky to take off her clothing while she was in the bathroom and then sexually molested her. For the past week, Vicky had been complaining of burning upon urination which was accompanied by pain and some irritation in her perineal area. Additional history revealed that Mrs. Burrows had treated Vicky for recurrent perineal irritation over the past year. Treatment had been with petroleum jelly as well as vitamin A and D ointment and had resulted in some resolution of Vicky's symptoms. A review of any probable related symptoms and past historical information were unremarkable and non-contributory. Vicky's growth and motor skills were age appropriate, but her physician did note her limited affect and moderate delay in her language and social skills.

The Burrows immediate family consisted of Mr. and Mrs. Burrows, Vicky, and cousin George. George had been living with Vicky's family for the past year because of difficulties he had encountered in his own home with his father. George had been sent to live with the Burrows family because George's parents believed that a change in George's environment would do him good, because it was likely that Vicky's father would not let George "get away with anything." On the morning following the alleged molestation, George "moved out" of the Burrows' home.

The Burrows' home, although clean and well kept, was the sole responsibility of Mrs. Burrows, even though she worked full-time as a waitress at a local pancake house. Vicky's father had worked as a telephone repairman at the same job for the past 15 years. He admitted to having a bad temper and insisting on strict discipline. Mr. Burrows stated that his relationship with his family was good, although he did admit to frequent arguments and fights with Mrs. Burrows, but considered these to be normal in any family. The Burrows family had continuously been short of money. The Burrows' credit had been poor, and they had been trying to pay off delinquent credit card accounts.

Vicky's interview was brief. She refused to maintain eye contact with the doctor or her father, nor would she answer any questions. Mr. Burrows remained in the examination room and only after repeated requests did he step into an adjoining area. Even then he continued to return to the examination room at frequent intervals.

Vicky's physical examination was essentially unremarkable except for her perineal area which showed intense redness most marked immediately surrounding the entry to her vagina. There were several abrasions noted on her right labia majora and a small scar on her left labia majora. Several bruises in various stages of healing were noted around her vaginal opening. The distance between Vicky's labia appeared subjectively increased and the measured distance between her labia was slightly greater than 6 mm. The remainder of Vicky's physical findings were normal except for a slight decrease in her rectal tone. Her laboratory evaluation consisted of several routine blood tests and trimucosal (throat, vagina, rectum) bacterial cultures for *Neisseria gonorrheoae* and *Chlamydia trachomatis*. Gonococcal organisms were detected in all three areas cultured and *Chlamydia trachomatis* was identified in specimens obtained from Vicky's vaginal and rectal areas.

A report of suspected child sexual abuse was initiated by the examining physician due to the abnormal findings present in Vicky's physical examination. The findings were further substantiated by the positive gonorrhea and chlamydia cultures. The state social service agency accepted the report, and, based on the physician's findings and the protective agency's investigation, indicated the report. The physician, state protection agency worker and state's attorney agreed that it would be helpful to obtain bacterial cultures for *Neisseria gonorrheoae* and *Chlamydia trachomatis* from the potential perpetrators. A court order directing that these cultures be done was obtained. Subsequently, cultures from Vicky's mother and cousin were negative for both organisms, however, cultures obtained from Vicky's father were positive for both *Neisseria gonorrheoae* and *Chlamydia trachomatis*.

At the juvenile court trial it was determined (in large part due to the medical evidence) that the most likely perpetrator was Vicky's father. He was "removed" from the home and a "no contact" order was issued.

Vicky's infections were treated with antibiotics and repeat cultures showed that the organisms had been eradicated. She was referred to an occupational therapy program for developmental stimulation. Vicky and her mother were also referred to a family therapist for assistance in dealing with Vicky's anger and depression. During subsequent visits to her pediatrician, she seemed happier and more spontaneous. By six years of age, her language and personal social skills had improved and she was felt to be developing appropriately. The family therapist, working in conjunction with a state protective agency worker, the physician, and Vicky's mother, felt that Vicky was making significant progress.

The case of Vicky Burrows demonstrates the potential input of the medical community in at least four areas: (1) the initial identification of the incest victim, (2) the initiation of the child sexual abuse report and referral of the patient to "the protective system," (3) the assessment of both the patient and her family, (4) initial disposition/management of the patient and long-term follow up (medical and interdisciplinary).

Vicky was brought to her pediatrician because of her physical injuries. In incest patients in whom physical abnormalities are present, the first professional to have contact with the victim is often a physician. Child victims, however, often enter the system following identification by other professionals. This alternate route is especially true if no obvious physical ailment is detected and/or the suspicion of sexual molestation is based on a report by the child or caretaker. Under these circumstances, medical evaluation is all too often omitted or delayed due to the limited lines of communication between the medical and non-medical systems and agencies. Because of this absence of direct interchange, which is often exacerbated by the unavailability of adequately trained personnel, information needed for the proper substantiation (assessment and evaluation of potential physical abnormalities and/or laboratory abnormalities) for both medical treatment and court purposes remains undetected. This absence or underutilization of an important additional safety net for children and families results in numerous cases of incest remaining unrecognized and/or inadequately documented and treated. The establishment of an ongoing dialogue, occurring at multiple layers within each organization, and accompanied by joint efforts to coordinate referral patterns will alleviate many of the recognized problems. In Illinois, the Liaison Division of Medical Education and Consultation has been established by a group of physicians in cooperation with the Illinois Department of Children and Family Services (Levy et al., 1984). The intent of this Liaison Divison has been to establish regional medical consultants to act as resources in cases of child abuse for social service workers, non-medical therapists and local physicians. This division also provides ongoing continuing education on matters related to child abuse/neglect as well as acting as a conduit for communication between physicians and the Illinois Department of Children and Family Service workers.

It has only been within the last several years that the medical community has become aware of and sensitive to the problems of child sexual assault. Prior to this time, physicians functioned with a limited knowledge base due to the lack of formal education offered in their training on issues of child abuse and sexual molestation. Often young physicians would have their first experiences in these areas during their residencies or upon their entry into private practice. Medical schools had rarely incorporated issues of child abuse or dysfunctional families into their formal curricula. This problem was exacerbated by the paucity of experienced clinical faculty available and capable of teaching the subtleties and complexities involved in cases of incest. The closing of these gaps in formal training and clinical experience are only now becoming priorities in the education of our future physicians.

Increasing awareness by the lay public and professional communities, concomitant with the apparent increase in cases of incest have emphasized the need for medical input into the evaluation and disposition of these cases. These pressures, along with initiatives such as that begun by the American Medical Association Panel designated to study child abuse and develop guidelines, have resulted in requirements for ongoing medical education in the diagnosis and management of these children and families. Clinical curricula are being developed which utilize problem-based, self-directed study to fill this need, such as the case study exemplified in this chapter. Problem-based learning curricula are adaptable not only to the medical profession at all levels of education (medical school, residency, post residency), but equally to non-medical professional groups.

Once the hurdle of the adequate identification of the child victim has been resolved, the issues of appropriate systematic handling of reports and treatment alternatives is necessary. It is apparent that formal referral patterns to and between appropriate agencies and professional groups are still in their infancy and require significant attention by all concerned to remain functional. Gaps in this system tend to result in discontinuity in patient care and potentially a tertiary abuse of the patient and family. The resultant mayhem causes frustration for all concerned professionals.

In the case of Vicky Burrows, physical and laboratory abnormalities were present and readily identified by her pediatrician. This case focuses on a pediatrician who was knowledgable in both the subtle and obvious physical abnormalities of incest, thereby making case identification appear easy. Many cases of incest, however, present to the professional with subtler findings than in Vicky's case. A definitive diagnosis or suspicion then becomes extremely difficult and is often dependent on statements made by the child or caretaker, or more commonly, upon subtle and unusual behavioral changes manifested by the child. A high index of suspicion on the part of the physician or other professional as well as a belief in the statement made by the child is required for any adequate assessment and appropriate disposition to take place. Once a victim such as Vicky has been identified, physicians and other professionals are often faced with the problems of appropriate referral and resources. At the present time, physicians are familiar with only a standard medical format of referral patterns. Few multi- or interdisciplinary approaches to the assessment and management of these patients exist in private practice. This lack of any interdisciplinary referral pattern exacerbates the problem of adequate management. The development of hospital-based and community-based interdisciplinary teams, functioning within a coordinated local and regional program along with the development of local and regional referral centers, will provide resources for numerous community services and improved management for the child and family. Pediatricians and family practitioners are in an excellent position to not only increase the number of children entering the system, but to do so in a sensitive, temporally appropriate fashion. These physicians also are often less threatening to both the child and family than other members of the community system of responses. They therefore may be able to intervene therapeutically even at the point of identification, where previously only an aura of accusation and punishment were present. As with Vicky Burrows, the coordination of information and collection of evidence in tandem with a cooperative posture by the physican, social service agency, and judicial system facilitated the collection of information. This resulted in optimal flow through the system while minimizing trauma to the child and family.

The physician may act not only as one of the gatekeepers in this system, but is often in a unique position to assess the child's sexual victimization by incorporating his or her knowledge of medicine (physical and behavioral child development) and the family as a unit. Innovative methods and tools of assessment are rapidly being developed and incorporated into the armamentarium of health care professionals. The pediatrician and family practitioner are often seen by the family and child as non-threatening advocates. They have the ability to obtain and interpret information not only collected during their medical evaluations, but also from external sources, such as the child's school. Information from other individuals who have evaluated the child's behavior may be available and included with the physician's finding, thereby allowing the integration of multiple levels of knowledge.

The physician with experience in child sexual abuse cases can interpret not only the findings brought to his or her attention upon presentation of the child, but also can assess certain crossover injuries, injuries not directly pertaining to sexual abuse, but often demonstrative of other forms of abuse (Levy, 1985). A comprehensive examination of the victim of incest performed by the experienced physician may reveal not only overt trauma, but other suggestive findings such as an interlabial separation greater than expected for age or changes in anal sphincter tone (Cantwell, 1983; Rimsza et al., 1982). The presence, staging and location of bruises and/or other signs of injury may provide valuable evidence in a process intended to protect the child. Specific laboratory tests may, on occasion, be the only available concrete evidence that will attest to the child's allegations. Accurate techniques for the culture and microscopic demonstration of sexually transmitted diseases such as *Neisseria gonorrhoeae*, *Chlamydia trachomatis*, and *Herpes genitalis* have been developed. The mere presence of these organisms in a prepubertal child may substantiate an allegation of child sexual abuse (Beilin, 1931; Neinstein et al., 1984; American Academy of Pediatrics, 1983; Rettig, 1984).

The physician may also occupy a unique position in his or her ability to monitor patients and families over time. The role of the pediatrician and family practitioner in tracking the longitudinal development of children is a time-honored practice and occurs with regular frequency. Parents rarely need to be convinced of the need for ongoing health maintenance visits for their children. These visits are easily integrated with an evaluation of the therapeutic success of various intervention programs including parent education and family therapy.

In summary, the medical community has the ability and responsibility to function within a multi- and interdisciplinary system responsible for the assessment and ongoing treatment of incestuous families. The individual physician can readily fulfill his/her role as a patient care provider and an advocate for children, while at the same time adding very necessary components to the social service and legal communities. These tasks recognize the role of physicians in four major areas: facilitating access to therapists and social service agencies; performing comprehensive, evaluative assessments of the victimized child; incorporating knowledge of medical illness, child development, and obtaining pertinent laboratory evidence; and assisting in the disposition and follow-up of cases.

The increasing recognition of the need to educate and interface the medical communities with the judiciary and social service systems may be paramount in our success in recognizing and treating incest victims. An increasing awareness of the roles and the subsequent cooperation between the various community agencies are fundamental in integrating the medical and psychosocial well-being of the victim and the family. These tasks are multilayered and provide a foundation for improved communication and resources. They also define the role of the medical community in a partnership with the social service and judicial communities whose combined responsibility is to protect the child from future abuse and ensure the child a nurturant environment.

ACKNOWLEDGEMENT

The authors wish to thank Mr. Gordon Jonson, Director, Illinois Department of Children and Family Services for his support in the development of the Liaison Divison of Medical Education and Consultation. The Liaison Divison of Medical Education and Consultation was made possible by a grant from the Illinois Department of Children and Family Services in order to provide medical consultation to the physicians and social welfare workers of Illinois and to educate physicians and other professionals on matters related to child abuse and neglect.

REFERENCES

American Academy of Pediatrics, Committee on Early Childhood, Adoption and Dependent Care (1983). Gonorrhea in prepubertal children. *Pediatrics*, 71, 553.

Beilin, L. M. (1983). Gonorrheal urethritis in male children. *Journal of Urology*, 25, 69–84.

Cantwell, H. B. (1981). Sexual abuse of children in Denver, 1979: Reviewed with implications of pediatric intervention and possible prevention. *Child Abuse and Neglect*, 5, 75–95.

Cantwell, H. B. (1983). Vaginal inspection as it relates to child sexual abuse in girls under thirteen. *Child Abuse and Neglect*, 7, 171–176.

Finkelhor, D. (1984). *Child sexual abuse*. New York: The Free Press.

James, J., Womack, W., and Strauss, F. (1978). Physicians' reporting of sexual abuse of children. *JAMA*, 240, 1145.

Levy, H. B., and Sheldon, S. H. (1984). A partnership between medicine and social service: A multidisciplinary approach to the primary, secondary and tertiary prevention of child abuse and neglect. Paper presented at the Fifth International Congress on Child Abuse and Neglect, Montreal, September 16–18.

Levy, H. B. Crossover injuries. Unpublished data.

Neinstein, L. S., et al., (1984). Nonsexual transmission of sexually transmitted disease: An infrequent occurrence. *Pediatrics*, 74, 67–76.

Rettig, P. J. (1984). Pediatric genital infection with *chlamydia trachomatis*: Statistically nonsignificant, but clinically important. *Pediatric Infant Diseases*, 3, 95–96.

Rimsza, M. E., and Niggemann, M. S. (1982). Medical evaluation of sexually abused children: A review of 311 cases. *Pediatrics*, 69, 8.

Woodling, B. A., and Kossoris, P. D. (1981). Sexual misuse: Rape, molestation, and incest. *Pediatric Clinics North America*, 28, 481–499.

Sexual Abuse:
Beyond the Family Systems Approach

David Finkelhor

Family systems thinking has been very important to the problem of sexual abuse. In many ways it, together with the women's movement, paved the road for professional recognition of a problem which had been apparently neglected and undetected for years. And its theories and concepts have been the mainstay of many mental health professionals who work with such families.

The family systems point of view aided the recognition of the problem of sexual abuse in two important ways among others. First, from its inception, the family systems approach has looked at symptomatic children and realized that they might be expressing problems originating with parents or other individuals in the family system (Foley, 1974). This orientation was crucial in preparing mental health professionals to see the possibility that disturbed-acting children might be acting disturbed because they were the victims of sexual abuse at the hands of family members.

Secondly, family systems theory served as an important antidote to the traditional psychoanalytic views, which had long obscured the problem of sexual abuse. Traditional psychoanalytic theory put its emphasis on the problem of children's unresolved incestuous impulses towards parents, not the parents' incestuous impulses toward the children (Masson, 1984). As long as sexually disturbed behavior in children was seen as an expression of the child's intrapsychic conflicts, the larger context of the problem was missed. By providing an alternative to the traditional intrapsychic view, family systems also helped create the possibility for recognizing sexual abuse.

The family systems approach also facilitated the recognition of sexual abuse by providing some of the first analyses that incorporated many of the current clinical observations. This analysis is typified by the following:

The preparation of this paper was made possible by a grant from the National Center for Child Abuse and Neglect (90CA 0936/01). It is one of a series of papers on sexual abuse and family violence from the Family Violence Research Program at the University of New Hampshire. The author would like to thank Linda Gott for help in preparation of this manuscript.

David Finkelhor, PhD, is Associate Director of the Family Violence Research Program, 128 Horton Social Science, University of New Hampshire, Durham, New Hampshire 03824.

53

We suggest that overt father-daughter incest depends upon: (1) an assumption by the daughter of the mother's role so general that the daughter has become the central female figure of the household; (2) an impaired sexual relationship between the parents, generating unrelieved sexual tension in the father; (3) an unwillingness by the father to act out sexually outside the family related to a need to maintain the public facade of a stable and competent patriarch; (4) a fear of family disintegration and abandonment shared by all protagonists, such that any arrangement appears preferable to family disintegration; (5) the conscious or unconscious sanction of the nonparticipant mother who must contribute to the assignment of the daughter in her place to care for the sexual, affectional and nurturant deprivation of the father. (Lustig, Dresser, Spellman, & Murray, 1966, p. 39)

This kind of analysis identified the features of what became the "classical" incestuous family, and gave a model to many therapists and child welfare officials who were desparately looking for clues with which to identify possible abusive families. Other concepts from family systems vocabulary, concerning the dynamics of secrecy, blame, enmeshment, and blurred boundaries (Kaufman, Peck, & Tagiuri, 1954; Kempe & Kempe, 1984), have also been widely utilized in understanding the often confusing behavior of members of incestuous families.

Such family systems concepts have also had a great influence on the process of therapy with and the rehabilitation of sexual abuse victims and their families (Giaretto, 1982; Sgroi, 1981). Despite the diversity of the treatment approaches proposed for dealing with sexual abuse, there is almost no approach which does not use family treatment in at least part of its program.

Yet for all the important contributions of the family systems approach to the problem of sexual abuse, the approach has come under increasing criticism (Conte, 1982). The criticisms have focused on the limited scope of the approach, its assumptions, its value judgements and its treatment implications. Research findings have not always confirmed its analysis. Concern that family systems analysis may have limitations in fully representing the sexual abuse problem has motivated a search for supplementary or broader analytic frameworks that might overcome some of the limitations.

What have been identified as some of the limitations of the family systems approach?

(1) One limitation concerns the scope of family systems analysis. The family systems approach has applied itself virtually exclusively to the problem of father-daughter incest. However, this is not the only kind of sexual abuse. In fact, it constitutes a surprisingly small proportion of all

sexual abuse cases. This is well illustrated by findings such as those of Diana Russell (1984), who conducted retrospective interviews with a random sample of adult women about childhood sexual abuse. As can be seen in Table I in that sample, parent-child sexual abuse constituted only seven percent of all the sexual abuse reported. Even if we limit ourselves to the *intrafamilial* sexual abuse, the parent-child incest still accounted for less than a quarter. The largest amount of sexual abuse was committed by persons known to the child, but not related, such as neighbors, family friends, teachers, ministers, baby sitters, etc. Within the family, the most frequent category of offenders was uncles. The family systems approach has not often addressed these other types of abuse.

Moreover, Russell's analysis was limited to women. Other studies (Finkelhor, 1979; 1984; Keckley Market Research, 1984) suggest that one out of three to one out of four cases of sexual abuse involves a male victim. With a few notable exceptions (Langsley, Schwartz, & Fairbairn, 1968), the abuse of males is not treated within the scope of the family systems approach either.

While surveys of unreported cases do show father-daughter abuse to be in the minority, this is not the same as the distribution of cases coming to the attention of professionals. In the distribution of reported child abuse, offenses by fathers do predominate. The figures from the National Incidence Study of Child Abuse and Neglect (Study Findings, 1981), for example, show that abuse by fathers and father substitutes constitutes 62% of these cases known to professionals. But even here we can see that there is much sexual abuse that is not like the classical model. One

TABLE 1: Relationship of Female Victim to
Perpetrator in Russell's Community
Survey of Sexual Abuse

Relationship	% all abuse (n = 647)
Parent/Step-parent	7
Other Relative	22
Friend	60
Stranger	11

important question is whether other forms of sexual abuse are *under*discovered in part because there is little theory to sensitize professionals about them. Unfortunately, family systems theory has not yet extended its analysis to include these other kinds of sexual abuse, and yet they are badly in need of some explanation.

(2) A second premise of the family systems approach that has come under some reconsideration concerns the strict distinction it has encouraged between intrafamilial and extrafamilial sexual abuse. This distinction is based on a presumption that dynamics in intrafamilial sexual abuse will be very different because they involve more intense betrayal of the child and more serious conflicts of loyalty among family members. This division of the field into intrafamily and extrafamily sexual abuse has some justification, but it can be overdrawn. Some extrafamilial sexual abuse has dynamics similar to intrafamilial sexual abuse, and also vice versa. For example, when the child reports that a trusted family doctor has molested her, it can provoke the same crisis of loyalty in parents and family that occurs when a child reports that an uncle has been doing the same. When molesters are doctors, teachers, scout leaders, or next door neighbors, their position of trust vis-à-vis the child and the family can be in many cases closer than in the case of an uncle or a cousin.

This blurring of boundaries is reflected in some of the research. With the one exception of father/daughter incest, researchers have been unable to show clearly and consistently that intrafamily sexual abuse causes more trauma than extrafamily abuse (Browne & Finkelhor, 1986). This suggests that the simple dichotomy between intrafamilial and extrafamilial sexual abuse may not always be useful.

(3) Another question that has been raised is whether family systems approach gives an adequate account of the sources of offender behavior. The implication of much family systems analysis is that sexually abusive behavior grows out of a matrix of family dynamics, and that it is an adaptation to some type of whole family dysfunction, rather than a deviant proclivity in the father. This is a contention which could be but has not been subjected to enough empirical investigation. Some available findings suggest that such explanations may not be sufficient, however, and that there are broader sources to even father-daughter incest, including the possibility that many incestuous abusers would be inclined to abuse independent of family dynamics.

In the research on sex offenders, the question has usually been posed in terms of whether incestuous fathers have characteristics of pedophiles and other sex offenders who have a rather autonomous proclivity to abuse. It appears that they do to a larger extent than previously recognized.

For example, many incestuous fathers appear to engage in a substantial amount of extra-familial pedophilic behavior. Abel, Cunningham-Rathner, Becker, and McHugh (1983) find that 45% of incestuous abusers of girls were sexually involved with children outside their family as well as their own children. This research is important because it gained admissions about pedophilic behavior from abusers under conditions of absolute confidentiality. Under ordinary conditions where incest fathers are facing possible criminal charges, it is understandable that such admissions of other sexually deviant behavior are less likely to be made.

There are also findings which show that incestuous abusers are like other child molesters in having unusual patterns of sexual arousal to pictures of children (Abel, Becker, Murphy, & Flanagan, 1981) and pedophile-like expressions of erotic preference (Langevin, Handy, Russon, & Day, 1985), but there are dissenting findings on this matter as well (Paitich, Langevin, Freeman, Mann, & Handy, 1977; Quinsey, Chaplin, & Carrigan, 1979). Still other findings suggest that incest offenders have personality profiles and developmental histories akin to pedophiles (Langevin et al., 1985; Panton, 1979). In summarizing their study, Langevin et al., (1985) report, "The results suggest that incestuous fathers are a mixed group of pedophiles and gynephilic men, of emotionally disturbed and stable men, of violent criminals and noncriminals."

All these findings suggest that a simple family systems analysis of incestuous behavior may be too narrow in many cases. Such an analysis may need to be supplemented with an individual analysis of the offender which considers whether he has an ingrained deviant pattern of erotic preference, whether he has a pattern of emotional disturbance, and whether he has an extensive criminal history, all of which may contribute to the incest behavior.

These findings also have relevance for therapy. To the extent that the sources of incestuous abuse lie in the individual offender, family therapy may be inadequate for eliminating the abuse. Such therapy may have to be augmented by individual and group work directly with the offender.

(4) A final question about the family systems approach to sexual abuse concerns value judgements that seem to be contained in some versions of the analysis. Some critics have maintained that the analysis often puts "moral responsibility" for the abuse on the mothers (McIntyre, 1981). They cite statements such as this:

> Despite the overt culpability of the fathers, we were impressed with their psychological passivity in the transactions leading to incest. The mother appeared the cornerstone in the pathological family system. (Lustig et al., 1966)

In the context of a situation where a father has violated one of society's most serious legal and cultural prohibitions, such statements do seem to represent a harsh, inverted value judgement. Few experts in the field would disagree that in some cases of sexual abuse mothers may have poor relationships with their daughters, may be eager to have daughters take on some of their role responsibilities, may ignore signs that incest is occurring, or may even fail to act when confronted with irrefutable evidence of the incest. It is not clear in what proportion of father-daughter incest these dynamics exist, but even when they do, they are open to a variety of explanations.

As many commentators have pointed out, these circumstances do not warrant holding mothers morally responsible for the incest (Herman, 1981; McIntyre, 1981). The behavior of mothers in incest situations can be just as easily accounted for by seeing the mother as a victim herself—trapped in an oppressive role to begin with, and then faced with an impossible dilemma, which is easy to deal with via denial (Zaphiris, 1978).

Certainly not all analyses from the family systems point of view endorse the idea that mothers are the "cornerstone" of the incest family. The question is whether because of its focus on the contribution of the whole family, the analysis has an inevitable tendency to exaggerate the role of the mother.

AN EXPANDED MODEL

It should be possible to expand our analysis of sexual abuse beyond the limitations of the family systems approach while still maintaining some of its insights. To do that, I have proposed what I call a "four pre-conditions model of sexual abuse" (Finkelhor, 1984). The model is an attempt to bring together the variety of factors that have been found to contribute to the occurrence of sexual abuse both within and outside the family. I will briefly sketch the model and then discuss its relationship to the family systems analysis.

The model proposes that four preconditions must be fulfilled before sexual abuse can occur. (1) A potential offender needs to have some motivation to abuse a child sexually. (2) The potential offender has to overcome internal inhibitions against acting on that motivation. (3) The potential offender has to overcome external impediments to acting on that motivation. (4) The potential offender or some other factor has to undermine or overcome the child's resistance to sexual abuse. The model is displayed in the Figure 1.

Precondition 1

The model proposes that all individuals who sexually abuse have some motivation for becoming involved sexually with a child. The review of the literature on these motivations suggests that there are three compo-

FOUR PRECONDITIONS OF SEX ABUSE

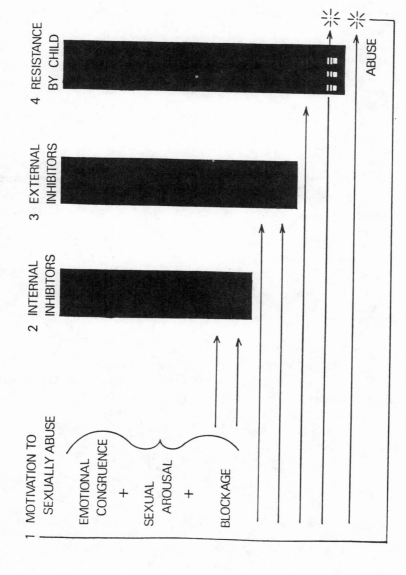

FIGURE 1. Four Preconditions of Sex Abuse

nents involved. The first is called *emotional congruence*, and it implies that relating sexually to the child is motivated by the satisfaction some important emotional need. There are a variety of such possible needs, but some that have been prominently noted are the desire to feel powerful and in control in sexual relationships (Howells, 1981; Groth, Hobson & Gary, 1982; Russell, 1984) or the need to remediate some early childhood abuse by re-enacting it in the role of the abuser (Howells, 1981; Groth, Hobson, & Gary, 1982).

The second element of motivation termed *sexual arousal* refers to the relatively well established fact that most sexual abusers, including many incest offenders, come to find children to be unusually sexually arousing to them (Freund, 1967; Quinsey, 1977). The source of this pattern of arousal is not well understood. In some cases it may involve biologic abnormalities (Berlin, 1982).

The third component, *blockage*, implies that connected to the motivation to sexually abuse is the fact that for many abusers alternative sources of sexual gratification are not available, either because of the abuser's internal conflicts or because of the absence of a partner. Research on child molesters and pedophiles does confirm shyness, sexual anxiety and social skills deficits (Glueck, 1965; Goldstein, Kant, & Hartman, 1973; Langevin et al., 1985) as well as relationship difficulties.

Not all these components are necessarily present in the motivational systems of all abusers, but there is some combination in all, and in many, all three can be found.

Precondition 2

The model gives emphasis to the fact that an individual may have many motivations to sexually abuse, but still may not do so because he recognizes that the behavior is wrong and illegal. Any account of sexual abuse must explain why these inhibitions are overcome in some but not in others. Such things as alcohol, stress, learned rationalizations, culturally weakened taboos and personality factors such as impulse disorder may explain the overcoming of these inhibitions, depending on the individual.

Precondition 3

The model also notes that there are many impediments in the environment that may inhibit sexual abuse. Many individuals who are motivated to sexually abuse do not do so because of these environmental restraints. These environmental restraints are undermined when children are poorly supervised by parents or isolated or when offenders have unusual opportunities for access to a child because the child is alone or housing conditions are crowded.

Precondition 4

Although it tends to be obscured from clinical attention, children themselves undoubtedly deter abuse in a variety of ways. Some children simply have personalities or demeanors that discourage abusers, by making it apparent that they are not the kind to be tricked or manipulated into sexual activities or the keeping of secrets. Other children actively resist the abuse by declining ploys, fighting back or running away. The model acknowledges that there are many things that may undermine children's resistance. For example, when children are emotionally insecure, lack knowledge about sex or have a relationship of great trust with the abuser, they may be more vulnerable because their motivation or capacity to resist the abuser is reduced.

Figure 1 illustrates the operation of the four preconditions model. It shows that the conditions come into play in a sequence. Emotional congruence, sexual arousal and blockage, in some combination, produce a motivation to become sexually involved with children. But of those individuals who are so motivated, only some overcome their internal inhibitions to act on these motives. Of those who overcome their internal inhibitions, only some overcome the external inhibitions. Then at Precondition 4, three things can happen. The child may resist in such a way as to avoid abuse. This is shown by the arrow stopping before precondition 4. A child may fail to resist and be abused or, as shown by the bottom arrow, the child may resist but have her or his resistance overcome through coercion as shown by the dotted line through precondition 4.

FAMILY SYSTEMS AND THE FOUR PRECONDITIONS MODEL

The four preconditions model is at a fairly high level of generality. One of the advantages of this is that it is adaptable to all types of sexual abuse. The four preconditions apply equally well to understanding abuse of boys and girls, abuse inside the family and outside, abuse committed by adolescents as well as adults, and so forth. Of course, different particular factors come into play in the various preconditions depending on the type of abuse. The development of sexual arousal to boys, for example, will be different from the development of sexual arousal to girls.

Because of its generality, too, the four preconditions model is not really in conflict with the family systems model. Rather it incorporates and expands upon most of the insights of the family systems approach. In fact, the family systems model can be seen as one particular instance of the four preconditions model, in this case, applying to the dynamics of father/daughter sexual abuse. When reformulated in terms of the four preconditions model, the family systems model looks like this:

Precondition 1. Motivation to abuse. Father may be motivated to take a sexual interest in his daughter because his relationship with his wife has deteriorated (blockage). Perhaps he sees in his daugher someone who has qualities similar to what he liked in his wife, but someone who can give him uncritical admiration and whom he can manipulate easily to fulfill his sexual and emotional needs (emotional congruence). Father may have himself been sexually abused, or as a result of his development has unusual needs to control and be powerful in sexual relationships (emotional congruence). He certainly has fantasized about his daughter and perhaps masturbated to these fantasies (sexual arousal).

Precondition 2. Overcoming internal inhibitions. Internal inhibitions against committing abuse are overcome either by alcohol or by a setback in his job or career aspirations. He rationalizes to himself that this is really an expression of love for his daughter, or that no great harm will be caused, or that committing incest is preferable to having an affair.

Precondition 3. Overcoming external inhibitions. External inhibitions against committing abuse are low because mother is not readily protective of daughter. Father may have cultivated a rivalry between mother and daughter. Or mother may be alienated from daughter for her own reasons. Daughter does not feel close to or readily confide in mother.

Precondition 4. Overcoming child's resistance. Daughter's resistance to father's advances is undermined because she trusts him, because she enjoys the attention, affection, and favored status. She may even feel she is holding the whole family together.

This is simply one example of how family dynamics can be incorporated within the four preconditions model. In other cases, other family dynamics may occur, but these also can be incorporated.

One of the valuable ways in which the four preconditions model expands on family systems analysis is in focussing more possible attention on dynamics within the offender. In some family systems analyses, the sexual unavailability of the wife is the only element offerred to explain offender motivation. This seems insufficient to explain incest given that sexual dysfunction and alienation afflict so many marital relationships that do not lead to sexual abuse. The four preconditions model puts focus on the emotional meaning of the sexual activity for the offender and also on the possibility that a deviant pattern of sexual arousal plays a role. Both these factors may imply an investigation into the background and socialization experiences of the offender. The four preconditions model also puts some focus on the issue of inhibitions, recognizing that only some fraction of men blocked from sexual gratification with wives, turn to their daughters as a substitute. Why a man might be disinhibited from violating such an important social taboo may also suggest individual-level exploration.

The four preconditions model is also helpful in putting issues of "responsibility" in perspective. In the four preconditions model, the behavior of mothers can indeed play a role, but the level of responsibility is more clear. It does appear that children with poor relationships with their parents, and particularly mothers, are at higher risk of victimization. This seems to be both because such children are less well supervised, do not have someone to confide in, and experience some degree of emotional deprivation which undermines their ability to resist abusers and their ploys. But these elements only come into play at Preconditions 3 and 4. They are only germane to the situation after a potential offender has taken some giant strides toward committing the offense, after he is embarked upon an anti-social train of events. If, for example, a father is well inhibited against engaging in sex with his daughter (Precondition 2) and if he has no motivation to sexually abuse (Precondition 1), then no contributing factor at Precondition 3 or 4 makes a difference. They are not in themselves capable of producing abuse. This seems to illustrate how effectively the "responsibility" for the abuse lies with the offender.

CONCLUSION

One of the most unusual features of the problem of sexual abuse has been the rapidity with which it came to public and professional awareness. Once considered a rather unusual mental health problem, in a matter of five years it has come to be recognized as a traumatic event in the lives of many children and families.

The last five years have also witnessed an enormous expansion in our knowledge about sexual abuse. Clinical experience and research knowledge have gained great momentum, as so many cases appear on the doorsteps of child welfare and mental health agencies.

Our theoretical grasp of sexual abuse needs to keep pace with this new level of experience and new level of knowledge. If they have taught us one thing it is that the problem is more varied and complicated than we once thought. Models that were developed at an earlier stage of our understanding need to be upgraded and expanded. Unfortunately, we have not developed theories with the complexity and depth to encompass the evidence, knowledge and experience we have amassed. Professionals with expertise in family systems theory need to join forces with those with other theoretical frameworks to build and test ideas adequate to the task of fully understanding this most disturbing problem.

REFERENCES

Abel, G., Becker, J., Murphy, W. D. & Flanagan, B. Identifying dangerous child molesters. In R. B. Stuart (Ed.), *Violent Behavior*. New York: Brunner/Mazel, 1981.

Abel, G., Cunningham-Rathner, J., Becker, J. V., McHugh. Motivating sex offenders for treatment with feedback of their psychophysiologic assessment. World Congress of Behavior Therapy, Washington, D.C., December, 1983.

Berlin, F. S. Sex Offenders: A biomedical perspective. In J. Greer & I. Stuart (Eds.), *Sexual aggression: Current perspectives on treatment* (Vol. 1): Victim treatment (Vol. 2): New York: Van Nostrand Reinhold, 1982.

Browne, A. & Finkelhor, D. The Impact of child sexual abuse: A Review of the research. *Psychological Bulletin*, 1986, 99: 66-77.

Conte, J. Sexual Abuse and the Family: Unraveling the Myths. Paper delivered at the Second National Conference on the Sexual Victimization of Children, Washington, D.C., May, 1982.

Finkelhor, D. *Sexually Victimized Children*. New York: Free Press, 1979.

Finkelhor, D. *Child Sexual Abuse: New Theory and Research*. New York: Free Press, 1984.

Foley, V. D. *An Introduction to Family Therapy*. New York: Grune & Stratton, 1974.

Freund, K. Erotic preference in pedophilia. *Behavioral Research and Therapy*, 1967, 5: 339–348.

Giaretto, H. *Integrated treatment of child sexual abuse*. Palo Alto: Science and Behavior Books, 1982.

Glueck, R. C. Pedophilia. In R. Slovenko (Ed.), *Sexual behavior and the law*. New York: Harper & Row, 1965.

Goldstein, M. J., Kant, H. S. & Hartman, J. J. *Pornography and sexual deviance*. Los Angeles: University of California Press, 1973.

Groth, N. A., Hobson, W. & Gary, T. The child molester: Clinical observations. In J. Conte & D. Shore (Eds.), *Social work and child sexual abuse*. New York: Haworth, 1982.

Herman, J. *Father-Daughter Incest*. Cambridge: Harvard, 1981.

Howells, K. Adult sexual interest in children: Considerations relevant to theories of etiology. In M. Cook & K. Howells (Eds.), *Adult sexual interest in children*. New York: Academic Press, 1981.

Kaufman, I., Peck, A. & Taguiri, C. K. The family constellation and overt incestuous relations between father and daughter. *American Journal of Orthopsychiatry*, 1954, 24: 266–279.

Keckley Market Research, *Sexual Abuse in Nashville*. Nashville, unpublished report, 1984.

Kempe, R. S., & Kempe, C. H. *The common secret: Sexual abuse of children and adolescents*. New York: W. H. Freeman and Company, 1984.

Langevin, R., Day, D., Handy, L., & Russon, A. E. Are incestuous fathers pedophilic, aggressive and alcoholic? In R. Langevin (Ed.) *Erotic Preference, Gender Identity and Aggression in Men*. Hillsdale, N.J: Lawrence Erlbaum Associates, 1985.

Langsley, D. G., Schwartz, M. N. & Fairbairn, R. H. Father-son incest. *Comprehensive Psychiatry*, 1968, 9: 218–226.

Lustig, N., Dresser, J. W., Spellman, S. W. & Murray, T. B. Incest. *Archives of General Psychology*, 1966, 14: 31–40.

Masson, J. M. *The assault on truth: Freud's suppression of the seduction theory*. New York: Farrar, Straus, & Giroux, 1984.

McIntyre, K. Role of mothers in father-daughter incest: A feminist analysis. *Social Work*, 1981, 26: 462–466.

National Center for Child Abuse and Neglect (NCCAN) *Study findings: National study of incidence and severity of child abuse and neglect*. Washington, D.C.: DHEW, 1981.

Panton, J. MMPI profile configurations associated with incestuous and non-incestuous child molesting. *Psychological Reports*, 1979, 45: 335–338.

Paitich, D., Langevin, R., Freeman, R., Mann, R., & Handy, L. The Clarke SHQ: A clinical sex history questionnaire for males. *Archives of Sexual Behavior*, 1977, 6: 421–435.

Quinsey, V. L. The assessment and treatment of chid molesters: A Review. *Canadian Psychological Review*, 1977, 18: 204–220.

Quinsey, V. L., Chaplin, T., Carigan, W. Sexual preference among incestuous and non-incestuous child molesters. *Behavior Therapy* 10: 562–565, 1979.

Russell, D. *Sexual exploitation: Rape, child sexual abuse, and sexual harassment.* Beverly Hills: Sage, 1984.

Sgroi, S. An approach to case management. In *Handbook of clinical intervention in child sexual abuse.* Lexington, MA: Lexington Books, 1981.

Zaphiris, A. *Incest; Crime with Two Victims.* Chicago; National Committee for prevention of Child Abuse and Neglect, 1978.

PART II: TREATMENT OF INTRAFAMILY SEXUAL ABUSE

A Systemic Model
for the Treatment of
Intrafamily Child Sexual Abuse

Mary Jo Barrett
Cece Sykes
William Byrnes

The purpose of this paper is to describe a comprehensive model for the treatment of intrafamily sexual abuse. The model has been developed over a twelve year period by several teams of therapists at Midwest Family Resource, in Chicago. Over two hundred and fifty families and individuals involved in incestuous relationships have been treated during this time period. A formal outcome study is presently being conducted, but the preliminary results indicate the program is highly successful in ending the abuse and allowing the families to remain together. The program has a recidivism rate of about 2 percent.

Intrafamily sexual abuse is a phenomenon that is currently receiving an abundance of both popular and professional attention. This increase in concern brings with it a proliferating number of articles and books that describe and explore the problem. There have been very few descriptions, however, of effective treatment programs which attend to the therapeutic needs of each individual family member, the family as a whole, and to the needs of society. The model outlined in the following pages is a description of a comprehensive program that works with all of the systems that are involved in the sexual abuse, before and after the molestation.

Mary Jo Barrett, Cece Sykes and William Byrnes are with the Midwest Family Resource, Chicago, Illinois.

The program is a systems-oriented treatment approach which operates on the premise that intrafamily sexual abuse is attributed to and maintained by a variety of interconnecting systems, family, individual, and societal. This conceptual framework is derived from the work of the structural (e.g., Minuchin, 1974) and strategic (e.g., Haley, 1976; Watzlawick et al., 1974) schools of family therapy. Using a framework and techniques from this structural/strategic orientation, our program works to change the structure of the family, reduce the dysfunctional behavioral patterns which have contributed to the abuse, and improve the family's communication patterns.

Our treatment program is divided into three stages, as seen in Figure 1. It is useful to conceptualize therapy in stages as this allows a therapist, court personnel, state caseworkers, and family members to have a clear understanding of the process of treatment. The use of therapeutic stages also permits the family to set and attain goals clearly. The general concepts and titles of the following three stages have been used in a model to treat other serious problems, such as anorexia nervosa and bulimia (Schwartz et al., 1984).

The stages of our program are as follows: (1) *Creating a Context for Change*. This stage concentrates on the assessment of the problem and lays the foundation for the ongoing treatment; (2) *Challenging Patterns and Expanding Alternatives*. Here we focus on helping the members solve dysfunctional behavioral sequences and choose new avenues of behavioral and emotional expression; and (3) *Consolidation*. This final stage cements the changes that have taken place and addresses future potential problem areas.

STAGE 1—CREATING A CONTEXT FOR CHANGE

Stage 1 of the program is designed to help the family begin to build an environment which allows enough flexibility so that eventually the members can function with no threat of abusive behavior. During this stage, we work intensely to coordinate services among the various agencies involved, begin a series of therapeutic interventions, and work actively on the ubiquitous denial of some or all family members.

Coordination of Services

During the first stage of treatment, the program emphasizes a high degree of involvement between our agency and the legal and state systems. An organized, clearly structured relationship is built and nurtured among these different staffs. Ongoing communication is mandatory and mutual goals whenever possible are established. A strong and consistent relationship enables productive conflict resolution. It is impor-

FIGURE 1

The Treatment Model

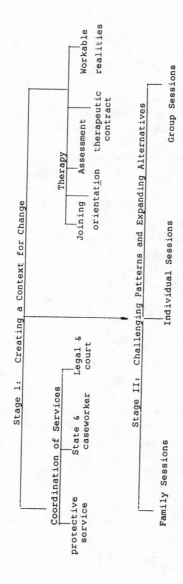
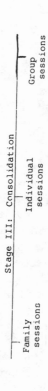

tant that the relationship between these agencies does not mirror the family's symptoms, such as rigidity or chaos. We pay particular attention to: (1) The pre-therapy investigation and protective service plan; (2) The ongoing role of the state and its caseworkers; and (3) The role of the legal and court system.

Pre-Therapy Investigation

Normally there is a lapse of time between the disclosure of the abuse and the referral to therapy. During this lapse an investigation and decision about the protective placement of the child takes place. We try to remain informed and involved in the protective service plan for each family that will be seen at our center. We help the protective service worker develop those criteria which will help make the difficult decision as to who, if anybody, should leave the home during the course of therapy.

This dilemma involves essentially four options. The first is to allow the family to remain intact. This requires a rare combination of emotional and protective qualities in the family. No violence has occurred, no substance abuse is present, acknowledgement and expression of emotions regarding the abuse is evident and a subjective opinion that safety is assured, are the elements involved in this decision. Because this option has the most risk associated with it and involves no immediate aversive consequences for the abuse, it is rarely recommended.

The second option is to remove the abusing parent and leave the child in the home. This is the option of choice whenever possible. We recommend this when the parent and child are willing to realistically address their relationship and its problems. At the same time, the non-abusive parent must be clear on her or his responsibility in protecting the child from further abuse. Finally, by being removed from the home the abusing parent receives a consequence for his or her behavior.

The third option is to arrange for protective custody of the child outside the home while the abusing adult remains in the home. This is a choice which is not usually recommended, since it inflicts a great amount of suffering on the abused child. It may further victimize the child by suggesting through the placement that the abuse was her or his fault. However, this option might be exercised if it were felt that the abusing parent would still be permitted back into the home by the non-abusing parent, even if court-ordered not to do so, and that the child then might be in danger of further abuse.

The final option is to remove both the abusing parent and the child from the home. This extreme measure is recommended when it is obvious that the non-abusive parent neither accepts any responsibility for their role in the problem, nor demonstrates a desire or ability to protect the child from further abuse. This option is used to maximize physical safety and minimize emotional rejection for the child.

The placement outside the home is handled delicately by our staff and the protective service agency. It is decided upon immediately, and all persons involved are clear on the arrangement and goals for the placement, as well as the criteria involved for the change in the living situation. The placement includes a highly responsible foster family or relative, who is, when possible, included in the therapeutic process. The risk that the child may become entangled in another web of complicated and conflictual relationships is great and obviously detrimental to the child and the therapy. We try to avoid this risk at all costs.

Coordination With the Caseworkers

Our program requires ongoing communication with the state caseworker on at least a monthly basis. Reports are written on the status and progress of the case quarterly. At the onset of treatment the family meets with our agency staff and the state agency. At this meeting the treatment plan and investigation is discussed, and tentative goals are explored. This meeting also focuses on the differing roles of the caseworker and the therapist. Families who are in the midst of the crisis of discovery are often confused by the number of agencies involved, so all necessary steps are taken to alleviate this confusion.

Coordination With the Courts

The role of the court system is clearly defined in this stage of therapy. For many families the authority of Juvenile/Family Court is sufficient to ensure compliance with casework planning. In this role the legal system is viewed as an ally in the therapeutic process; not only can the law provide structure, but it can take on the role of authority while the therapist acts as the advocate. The criminal court may be involved if the family is resistant to treatment, if the family is so chaotic that there is an increased risk that the abuse will continue, or if there is a history of sexual, criminal or violent behavior of the offender. Criminal probation or incarceration may be necessary in order to protect the child and the community. Our therapists are continually updated on all criminal proceedings and if possible maintain contact with all incarcerated clients.

In creating a context that is conducive to change, the persons designated as change agents must work effectively together. This does not mean all the different systems must be in total agreement It does mean, however, that they operate in an atmosphere that encourages communication, conflict resolution, and the exploration of alternatives. The family can not be expected to behave in a constructive manner without the coordination of the outside systems. The therapist must early on coordinate this cooperative effort to avoid later pitfalls that can deter therapy.

Therapeutic Techniques

There are six therapeutic procedures which we use in Stage 1: joining; orientation session; assessment sessions; establishing a therapeutic contract; the family structure session; and the apology session. For the sake of convenience and clarity, these procedures are described separately; in the program, they occur concurrently. The decision which intervention to use at what time is predicated upon the therapist's style and the nature of the case.

Joining

Joining (Minuchin, 1974) is the establishment of a positive therapeutic relationship. The therapist communicates to the family an understanding of the complexities of incest, that everyone has a role in making the situation better, and that change is possible. Joining also involves the therapist being seen as an ally. The procedure requires the therapist to accommodate to the family's style and structure during this initial period, which may be difficult for someone who has not explored personal values around incest. The operation of joining begins with the first phone call and takes place in every session throughout therapy. These first steps build the trust that will allow the therapist to later confront and challenge the family.

The Orientation Session

This session includes an overview of the therapy, a further explanation of the different agencies involved, an exploration of the protective service issues and how they will be instituted, and an outline of the rules of treatment. Some issues typically addressed are: roles and responsibilities of the professionals involved, rules regarding visitation of family members, the stages and the techniques of therapy, and expectations regarding attendance and behavior in family, individual, and group sessions.

Family Assessment

Our formal assessment procedure (described in Trepper and Barrett) focuses on family structure, such as adaptability, hierarchy, and cohesion; and family communication patterns. The assessment also determines the level of functioning of each individual family member.

This is accomplished through family and individual sessions, and psychological testing when necessary. These sessions determine current psychological status, level of depression, the presence of suicidal ideation, and the assessment of substance abuse. Further, we explore relevant historical information; family of origin factors; sexual functioning of the husband and wife; and past occurrences of sexual, physical, or emotional abuse. Every effort is made to bring together as many of the family members as possible, including extended family, to fully assess their current functioning.

The Therapeutic Contract

The development of a therapeutic contract allows the family to become more directly involved in the treatment process. Each member is encouraged to prioritize individual and family treatment goals. These goals need not focus solely on the sexual abuse. Problems that the family experiences, such as parenting difficulties, employment, school related issues, and social functioning are also valid goals. Because our program attempts to integrate many areas of family life, the treatment goals reflect this.

Family Structure Session

The family's view of themselves after the discovery and at the beginning of treatment is very negative and not conducive to therapy. They see themselves as sick, hopeless, and persecuted failures. We work to help the family change this deficit view to one that is based not on weaknesses but on strengths. We help the family see themselves as capable and competent human beings. We want the clients to understand their problems in a manner that encourages change and hope.

The purpose of the "Family Structure Session" is to help the family begin to answer the question, "How did this happen to us?" The session provides a common language for the family and the therapist when discussing the sexual abuse. Structural maps are drawn for the family illustrating how molestation occurs when the family members cross generational boundaries (see Trepper and Barrett, Figure 2, p. 19). This crossing of boundaries results in the parent and child functioning as if they were peers. They explore which structures apply to their family and in what ways they operate within the "wrong" generation. For example, the family discusses different family roles and role reversal in such areas as household chores, sibling care, and alliances during leisure time. The important component of this insight-based session is to help the family understand the functional role the incest played in their family. This session also emphasizes that the responsibility for safety and care of children belongs to the parents.

The Apology Session

The apology session is an opportunity for the family to express their current emotional state with respect to the sadness, remorse, and anger over the incest. It is also a time for them to express their hope about their future family functioning. The purpose of the Apology Session (described in Trepper) is fourfold: (1) It is a beginning to help alleviate the abused child's guilt; (2) It clarifies that the responsibility for the abuse is with the parents; (3) It promotes clearer and more direct communication; and (4) It helps restructure an incongruent hierarchy by having the parents be equally in charge during the session. The session occurs after several individual, as well as parental dyadic sessions. The Apology Session does not take place until the therapist is confident that the intervention will not have a detrimental impact on the child.

In Cases of Denial

Stage 1 described thus far has assumed the family members have admitted to the allegations of sexual abuse. We believe a therapist can not successfully progress to Stage 2 if there is active denial on the part of any or all family members. This does not mean that therapy must be terminated. It does mean the therapeutic strategies must be altered to accommodate the denial. We have identified at least four types of denial, which are presented in Table I.

Denial serves a protective function for the individual and the family. The therapist needs to understand the importance and the function of the denial in order to use it therapeutically. The clinician walks a careful

TABLE 1

Denial

Type	Parent	Child
Denial of Facts	"It never happened"	"It never happened"
Denial of Awareness	"I was drunk"	"I was asleep"
Denial of Impact	"It didn't harm her"	"It doesn't affect me"
Denial of Responsibility	"She came on to me"	"It was my fault"

balance between supporting the emotional need to deny and at the same time challenging the person who is denying to accept the reality of the sexual abuse.

The offending parent's denial is dealt with in a series of individual sessions. There is a constant challenge for them to look at themselves and the evidence against them. In these sessions we ask, somewhat paradoxically, "If it *were* true (and we are not now saying that it is), what do you fear would happen to you and your family?" Persistent denial is addressed through individual, group, and marital sessions, taking as much time as necessary. The couple sessions are particularly useful if the nonabusing parent believes the report. If the abusing parent continues to deny, however, we may suggest that legal counsel is needed rather than family therapy.

The spouse's denial of the offending parent's behavior reflects her or his fears of divorce, abandonment, and often poverty. This is particularly understandable if the spouse is a woman. Women often have to choose between the needs of their mate and the needs of their children; this problem becomes exacerbated in incest families. The therapist is sympathetic to this dilemma and yet challenges the client to take the responsibility of a parent.

The child who denies the initial report is usually protecting the family from what they perceive as threats from the outside community. The child is responding to verbal or nonverbal pressure from the parents and/or siblings to remain loyal to the family. We work directly with the child and family to help them find a new kind of loyalty without the threat of abuse. Individual sessions are mandatory for the child when any of the types of denial are present. Therapy is often the child's only source of validation and support.

Stage 1 of the program is completed when the therapist has accomplished the following: established a mechanism for ongoing network communication among the various agencies involved; joined with each family member; completed the assessment; established a therapeutic contract; and developed, through the Family Structure, Apology, and individual sessions, "workable realities" that allow the family the dignity and flexibility to grow inter- and intra-personally.

STAGE 2—CHALLENGING PATTERNS AND EXPANDING ALTERNATIVES

Sexual abuse takes place partially because a series of dysfunctional behavioral patterns has become established and difficult to break. Stage 2 of therapy helps to break these recursive sequences and open up vast numbers of functional alternatives from which to choose. These dysfunctional psychological patterns are established and maintained through many sources, such as family of origin, society, personality, and peer group. Consequently, the therapy must address these varying contexts and help the members change within these contextual restraints. This is accomplished through the concurrent utilization of family, group, extended family, and individual sessions.

Family Sessions

Family sessions address the dysfunctional repetitive interactional sequences that currently maintain the symptom. There are four areas that we address in these sessions over time; cohesion, adaptability, hierarchy, and communication.

Cohesion

Cohesion refers to the emotional bonding that family members have toward one another (Olson et al., 1979). Typically, the incestuous family is viewed as enmeshed, which refers to an excessive overinvolvement among family members. Because of this overinvolvement, any attempt at individuation by family members is met with the threat of abandonment. This threat is a constant source of anxiety to the individuals who are trying to separate, and a source of power for those trying to inhibit the change.

Interventions are designed to reduce the level of enmeshment while still allowing the family to retain the more positive aspects of their closeness. The common myths in enmeshed families, such as "We must solve all of our own problems," and "If someone disagrees with me he or she does not love me," is confronted. The therapist encourages family members to have privacy, and to develop outside-the-family relationships. Parents are encouraged to respond to their children in a way that is neither smothering nor rejecting.

Adaptability

Adaptability refers to the amount of flexibility to change a family typically demonstrates, and can range on a continuum from rigid to chaotic (Olson et al., 1979). Incest families tend to fall on either extreme. *Rigid* families display an extremely limited range of behaviors, especially when crisis occurs. These families tend to be "rule conscious," and often display rigid sex-role expectations. Rules such as "You always do what daddy tells you to," may to some extent contribute to inappropriate, unchecked sexual behavior. *Chaotic* families appear to be "ruleless" and "rulerless," and seem to have difficulties with the management of day-to-day activities.

For rigid families, the task for the therapist is to help the family operate more flexibly with regard to their roles and rules. For example, if mother has unquestioningly accepted the role of the supporter of father, and never disagrees with his ideas or decisions, then the therapist must unbalance this pattern. Through in-session tasks and homework assignments, the clinician helps the family see the benefits that will accrue when mother becomes an equal participant in decision making.

For chaotic families, the task for the therapist is to provide structure and organization for the family that will eventually be accommodated by their system. Consistent parenting is encouraged, and specific family tasks are assigned which strengthen more appropriate roles for the parents and children. Family rules are developed, not just around sexual behavior, but in all areas of family life. The therapist monitors the compliance to these rules by all members.

Hierarchy

Hierarchy refers to the graduated system of membership in the family. This system is usually defined by age, power, and roles. In healthy families, clear boundaries exist separating parents from children. In many incest families, these boundaries are blurred. This may permit a hierarchical shift "downward" by the adult into the children's generational domain, or "upward" by the child into the parents' domain.

The therapist's job is to challenge the incongruent hierarchies. Disciplining tasks are given to provide the parents with a sense of competence in their use of authority, without abuse. The children often exhibit initial resistance to their parent's new behavior. These negative reactions to more appropriate parenting is predicted early on in therapy, which seems to reduce the impact.

During the family sessions, the therapist directly intervenes whenever he or she witnesses an inappropriate shift in hierarchy, such as the child assuming the role of wife, or a parent assuming the role of child. Between-session assignments are made to promote a change in existing boundaries or establishing nonexistent ones. A mother and daughter, for example, might be given the task of spending time together. The identified child and siblings are given tasks to promote their peer relationship, such as going shopping together, or cooking a meal for the family together.

Communication

In incestuous families, communication is comprised of secrecy, poor conflict resolution, indirect and self-protecting messages, and an inability to communicate affectively. Interventions are designed to improve both instrumental and affective communication among family members. For example, the family is encouraged to communicate directly with one another, not through the therapist. The therapist punctuates the negative communication patterns and helps the family to establish a new style. Conflict resolution, negotiation, and compromise are all developed through standard communication exercises. Secrecy is always discouraged, while openness of communication is encouraged.

Individual Sessions

The purpose of the individual sessions is to allow individual family members to explore those issues which may be important to them. All individual sessions are coordinated with the family therapy, and usually provided by the family therapist.

Offender

Sessions with the offender focus on a number of issues. For example, if the offender has not formally admitted to the abuse, the clinician continues to challenge the need for the denial. Other clinical content focuses on the abuser's family of origin and psychosocial development. The therapist works with the person to develop a working hypothesis as to why the abuse took place. Current life concerns are examined particularly in the area of sex roles, and sexual feelings and behaviors. The client is challenged to establish personal goals and to continually reflect upon the barriers that previously inhibited his or her "healthy" functioning. In general, the goal of these sessions is to allow the client to examine the many complex factors that contributed to his abusive behavior.

Non-abusing parent

Individual sessions with the non-abusing parent focuses on those problems unique to her or him. This parent is often initially the one experiencing the most anxiety and/or depression which must be addressed directly. Also, there may be much guilt associated with what is perceived as their role in the abuse. The therapist works with the non-abusing parent to remove her or him from the role of secondary victim. An in-depth exploration takes place concerning feelings about the spouse, children, and herself. We also include a review of her family of origin to help identify the foundations of the patterns that contribute to the abuse.

Child

We provide individual sessions for the abused children to explore their feelings about the abuse, individuation, self-perceptions, and peer issues. The therapeutic strategies depend on the age of the children.

With children under the age of five it is most helpful to work primarily with play therapy and parent-child sessions in tandem. We use investigative techniques with anatomically correct dolls and coloring books. The purpose of this is not to simply have the children retell the story, but to serve as a vehicle by which the therapist can help the children learn to protect themselves and to rid themselves of guilt. We want the children to relearn trust and to realize intimacy is not damaging. The children are given permission to express their thoughts and feelings through play. Also during these sessions, age appropriate behavior is encouraged. The mothers are usually present and involved during these sessions.

Individual sessions for older children and adolescents focus on the affective areas of shame, guilt, depressions, and anger. Flashbacks and dreams are discussed, predicted, and normalized as part of the adjustment process. An attempt is made during these sessions to "devictimize" the children and to help them learn how not to be a victim in future interactions. The children define how they want their role in the family to change, such as more independence, less responsibility, less direct involvement with the problems of their parents, and a better relationship with their siblings. The therapist helps the children bring these issues constructively and safely to their families.

The therapist is often the children's major support system during this period of time; consequently he or she must not overprotect the children and must permit them to take appropriate risks. It is the balance between support and respect that we have found works the most effectively.

Marital Sessions

These sessions serve to establish boundaries around the marriage that did not previously exist. The marital sessions help the couple begin to make pragmatic decisions about their relationship. If there has been a decision to divorce then the emphasis remains on the divorce process and future parenting operations. If the couple is separated then the treatment helps them explore the alternatives of divorce or marriage. If the couple remains together, literally or figuratively, then the therapy focuses on improving their relationship directly.

No matter what the marital status, all couples come to understand how a dysfunctional marriage can contribute to intrafamily child sexual abuse. The dyad explores their repetitive sequences that promoted distance, such as problems in conflict resolution. The techniques used are similar to those of conventional marital therapy. The areas we most typically concentrate on include: conflict resolution; intimacy; communication patterns; sexuality; and long-term expectations of their marriage.

The therapist continually weaves the theme of sexual abuse into the sessions. When dealing with the sexual relationship of the couple, however, care is taken not to define any sexual problems that may be present as the primary cause of the sexual abuse. If a sexual dysfunction is present, we may include sex therapy for the couple in our treatment plan.

Sibling Sessions

Sibling sessions are used to help the children allay their fears, confusion, anger, and concerns regarding the molestation. In addition, these sessions help to reestablish the children into their generational ranks and relieve the non-abused children from any guilt or responsibility they are experiencing. The siblings often experience guilt because they did not protect the abused child, or because they had previous knowledge of the abuse and did not report it. They also may feel ashamed of the relief they experience not being the victims of the abuse.

Many non-abused siblings are angry because their family has been split-up, and they have to face public humiliation. Occasionally we have found siblings attempting to help and protect the family by displaying their own symptoms, such as acting-out. We view this as an attempt to distract the family from the sexual abuse. If the children are involved in sibling sessions then the function of their acting out behavior can easily be explored.

Group Sessions

The function of group sessions within a systems-oriented program is to expand and intensify the issues and alternatives developed in the family, marital, and individual sessions. Groups can be an important component to treatment because they can expedite the changes occurring in the family. It should be noted, however, that all of the group activity is coordinated with the family sessions. The emotional readiness of the individuals involved determines when to initiate the sessions in the overall treatment plan.

Our program recommends that at least the victim and the parents attend groups. As the need arises, we conduct groups for the couple, mother-child dyad, and father-child dyad. Auxiliary and self-help groups such as Alcoholics Anonymous, Ala-non, Ala-teen or church groups are also incorporated as part of our program. All of these group experiences can provide a safe context in which the clients can experiment with new interactional behaviors. The members are encouraged to risk and to challenge in the group and then to generalize these feelings and behaviors into their family and community at large.

STAGE 3—CONSOLIDATION

This final stage of our program seals the changes that have taken place thus far and explores potential problem areas in future functioning. In this stage, the families take on more responsibility for problem-solving, conflict-resolution and decision making. The communication in the sessions by this time should be clear, direct, and more constructive. The families should be able to articulate a problem that currently exists and discriminate between how they would have coped in the past and how they are coping presently.

Interventions are designed for supporting the families independence from therapy. Sessions become less frequent over time. The families are asked to predict potential future problems, particularly those relating to developmental transitions. Emphasis in these sessions is placed on coping skills and strategies. Some future problems are predicted, but the family is encouraged to return to therapy whenever needed for any problem. Therapy is seen now as a helpful resource, rather than a place where you are sent when you are in trouble.

The duration of the consolidation phase in family, individual and group sessions is based on the needs of the family and judgement of the therapist. Usually, this stage lasts about three months. The entire therapy process lasts between 12 and 18 months.

SPECIAL ISSUES

In running an effective program for the treatment of intrafamily sexual abuse we have found the following guidelines useful:

(1) *Inter- and intra-agency coordination of services is mandatory.* The family and the therapist can easily be caught in a complicated interactional web that can lead to the demise of effective treatment. The client is best viewed as the family, the law, the state, and the community.

(2) *It is essential to be aware of the values that different family members and community members uphold.* The community attitude can be one of disbelief, horror, and disgust about the event, and consequently little support may be given to the therapeutic agency. These attitudes need to be recognized and then planned for the treatment program.

(3) *Whenever possible, the use of co-therapy teams or ongoing supervision is essential.* As in all therapy, but particularly with sexual abuse, we need to be aware of our own attitudes, biases, and values. Because sexual abuse is as emotionally charged as it is, we highly recommend the use of therapy teams whenever possible. If this is not possible, then ongoing active supervision or consultation is essential. The

intensity of the problem and the treatment can become overwhelming and it is easy to become therapeutically "stuck." The team or colleague can provide support and can also help provide a new therapeutic direction. The therapist must not reflect the family's rigid patterns by becoming rigid themselves. This can be avoided by not working in isolation as the family once did.

SUMMARY

A comprehensive program for the treatment of intrafamily child sexual abuse has been described. This program is based on a family-systems model, but incorporates individual, family, and group therapy components. The major goal of the program is to reduce the likelihood of further sexual abuse by changing the family structure and communication patterns. It is recommended that all concerned agencies be included in the assessment, treatment planning, and therapy.

REFERENCES

Haley, J. (1976). *Problem-solving therapy*. San Francisco: Jossey-Bass.
Minuchin, S. (1974). *Families and family therapy*. Cambridge, Mass: Harvard University Press.
Olson, D. H., Sprenkle, D. H., and Russell, C. S. (1979). Circumplex model of marital and family systems I: Cohesions and adaptability dimensions, family types, and clinical applications. *Family Process*, 18, 3–28.
Schwartz, R., Barrett, M. J., and Saba, G. (1984). *Psychotherapy for anorexia nervosa and bulimia*. New York: Guilford.
Watzlawick, P., Weakland, J. H., and Fisch, R. (1974). *Change: Principles of problem formation and problem resolution*. New York: Norton.

Child Sexual Abuse:
Generic Roots of the Victim Experience

Carol R. Hartman
Ann Wolbert Burgess

Although progress has been made in the past decade in understanding the different levels of symptoms in children who have been sexually abused, there remains a knowledge gap with regard to the meaning of the abusing event and how that event is cognitively processed by the child. We believe it is critical to understand the structure of this experience for the child so that we may provide more meaningful interventions.

The purpose of this article is to present a conceptual framework for understanding the nature and structure of the abusing experience for the child-victim. In doing so, we will address: (1) the phases of sexual abuse and recovery, which will focus on the sequencing and time parameters involved in experiencing, disclosing, and recovering from sexual abuse; and (2) the manner in which the abuse is processed by the child, including the mediating mechanisms involved, how the child may encapsulate the trauma, the dissociative processes which may occur, and the patterned responses of victims to the event.

PHASES OF SEXUAL ABUSE AND RECOVERY

The various phases of sexual abuse and recovery elicit different responses from the child or adolescent victim, depending upon certain factors. These factors contribute to how successfully or unsuccessfully the child psychologically will handle the abuse.

Pre-Abuse Phase

The more social and psychological coping mechanisms are available to the child before the sexual abuse takes place the better the child is likely to handle the trauma of abuse. The factors that seem to be most important include: (1) the environmental supports available; (2) the quality of

Carol R. Hartman, R.N., D.N.Sc. is Associate Professor and Coordinator, Graduate Program in Psychiatric Mental Health Nursing, Boston College, Chestnut Hill, MA 02167.

Ann Wolbert Burgess, R.N., D.N.Sc. is the van Ameringen Professor of Psychiatric Mental Health Nursing, University of Pennsylvania School of Nursing, Philadelphia, PA 19104.

relationships with adults and siblings; (3) the child's psychological organization; and (4) the child's ego development.

Abuse Phase

The factors which appear most critical during this phase are: (1) the relationship of the assailant to the child; (2) the degree of violence, threat, and intimidation used; (3) the type of sexual and other physical acts; (4) the child's age; (5) the defenses and coping mechanisms used by the child throughout the assault period (including behavioral, cognitive, and psychological defenses); (6) the patterns of inhibition and disinhibition demanded of the child for survival in response to the abuser's aggressive and erotic behaviors; (7) the presence of multiple perpetrators; (8) the use of pornography; (9) the extent of distortion and bizarreness in the sexual activity; and (10) the symptoms manifested by the child. Obviously, the more of these factors which are present, the more difficult it will be psychologically for the child to manage.

Disclosure Phase

The crucial questions which need to be explored during this phase include: (1) Was the disclosure voluntary or forced? (2) How does the system respond to the child? This response could include physical examination, interviews about what happened, and contact with the criminal justice system, as well as family and extended social network response. (3) What type of contact does the child have with the perpetrator? If the perpetrator is a family member, such as parent or sibling, the impact of the social support system is important in how it shapes the victim's thoughts about himself or herself and the abuse experience. If the perpetrator is a stranger, has the stranger been apprehended? (4) Is the offender released after a period of confinement? (5) Does the offender attempt to threaten the child (which can occur in cases of group or sex ring involvement)? (6) How many symptoms of stress manifest themselves and what are the characteristics of these symptoms?

Post-Disclosure Phase

The critical questions which must be answered in determining how successfully the child will manage this phase include: (1) What life adjustments have been made? (2) How much disruption has there been in pre-assault life activities? (3) How are signs of aggression or avoidance handled by family or victim? (4) How is sexualized behavior dealt with by family and victim? (5) Has there been continuous goal-directed development in the child? and (6) To what extent does the family talk with the child about the abuse and about how the child is presently managing?

TRAUMATIC EVENT PROCESSING

It is critical when assessing a child's response to sexual abuse to understand the factors occurring at each of the above phases which will determine the degree to which the child can successfully manage the traumatic event. We will now present a model which we feel represents the specific mechanisms involved in the way the child cognitively processes the sexual abuse.

Pre-Abuse Conditions

As previously noted, the pre-abuse conditions can serve to indicate the child victim's strengths and vulnerabilities. In addition, they are often important factors in the child's recovery from the sexual abuse.

These conditions can be described as falling into one of three categories. The first, *early life history*, includes quality of relationships with adults and siblings, early socialization experiences, and social resources. The second, *pre-existing beliefs and values*, are those pertinent patterns of adaptation which allow for more effective coping. The third, *level of life stress conditions* incorporates how stressful the child's life is in ways that has an impact on the intensity of his or her reaction to the abuse.

Event

We use the term event to refer to the sexual activities and abuse that occurs between the child and the adult whether this abuse occurs only once or whether it continues over time. The event may include a wide range of behaviors including some of the following: dialogue and conversation about the victim's sexuality; physical sexual contact; the use of force, orders, and threats (including threats to life); and ploys used to guarantee secrecy and continuance of the sexual activity.

Informational Processing of the Event: The Mediating Mechanism

In considering the victim's post-abuse reactions, it is useful to think of cognitive-behavioral adjustment to a traumatic event as arising from the informational processing which occurred during the event. The presumption is that information is kept in active awareness until it can be placed in distant memory. That comes about when there is sufficient processing for the information to be stored. Successful counseling can facilitate this processing, allowing the victim to place the event in distant memory.

There is currently no empirical research on traumatic event processing by sexual abuse victims. The closest we have is research on wartime trauma, which will be briefly reviewed because of its similarity to child sexual abuse in duration, use of authority, and variance in impact. Researchers studying Vietnam War veterans have noted that a combination of brutal training, immersion in the horror of war, and a hostile homecoming have prevented the veterans from taking their expected place in society (Egendorf et al., 1981; Figley, 1979). Victim-survivor wartime trauma research has noted the many classes of variables (e.g., demographic, dispositional, and environmental) that affect how an individual experiences or assimilates a traumatic event.

The central feature of Post Traumatic Stress Disorder (PTSD), which is the stress pattern resulting from traumatization, is that the individual re-experiences the original trauma both unconsciously and consciously. This re-experience phenomenon is expressed in intrusive, uncontrolled, and disturbing thoughts and images; in dreams and nightmares; in dissociative states of consciousness; and in unconscious symbolic or behavioral re-enactments of the traumatic situation as either the victim or the aggressor (Horowitz, 1975).

One major difference between child sexual abuse and wartime trauma is, of course, the age of the individual experiencing the event. In child sexual abuse, the child's personality is forming; thus, the event intervenes with the child's developing ego. In the young adult going to war, the personality integration of the stress and trauma of combat and adjustment becomes a function of pre-existing personality and coping patterns.

The study of informational processing has given some clues to the intensity of the defensive adjustment made by children who are assaulted over a prolonged period of time. Their initial distress is subdued by a level of cognitive operations that allows the abuse activities to be stored partially in past memory. It is merely speculation as to what the child does cognitively to accomplish this, although it is assumed that dissociation, to be described later, plays an important role.

This information processing premise also suggests why disclosure is so upsetting to the child, as disclosure requires a breakdown of the defensive structures in order to retrieve or disclose the information. If disclosure comes from an outside source, the child may respond with distress and anger toward the outside person who reveals what is going on. The child's anger is defensive and protective of his or her adjustment to the long term abuse.

Encapsulation of the Event

A growing body of literature supports the premise that sexual abuse of children is a traumatic event having personal repercussions over time (Browne and Finkelhor, 1984). Of particular importance to child sexual abuse is that after the first expression of acute symptoms are manifested by the child, and no substantive response to the child's predicament follows, there is a quiescent period when the molestation still continues. It is during this period that the child must in some manner encapsulate the trauma of the abuse.

The encapsulation process has two components. First, silence is required by the offender about the abuse. Second, a defensive position is taken by the child to discuss and to avoid any possible detection. This defensive silence encloses the sexual abuse that is ongoing; the informational processing of the ongoing event holds the event in present memory.

This encapsulation process depletes the child's psychic energy and thus disrupts the continuity of development of other areas of the child's psychological make-up. Of particular concern is its impact on the victims' sense of right and wrong, their sense of self, their arousal capacities and their inhibition capacities, their awareness or lack of awareness of body states, their sense of personal power, and their self-comforting, self-preserving, and protective behaviors. There is also concern for the reality-mediating strategies used by the child to survive psychologically, cognitively, and (at times) physically.

Dissociation from Event

One way to understand the impact of sexual abuse on the child's developing personality structure is to analyze the development of the ego and the mechanisms of its defense. Ego as used here denotes that part of the personality that perceives, experiences, judges, and controls behavior. Ego development is involved with individual coping and adaptation processes. We find these concepts extremely useful in understanding impairments and gains in individual maturation.

During the past several decades major contributors to writings on ego psychology have included Anna Freud (1983), Heinz Hartmann (1948), and Erik Erickson (1950) among other contemporary theorists. Anna Freud (1983), among others, had emphasized that during normal ego development, in the battle for impulse control, developmental defects can take the place of regressive processes. This may be noted in an individual by a different rate of ego growth and a variance in the strength of the drives of sex and aggression. This state has the capacity to create internal disharmony, which the individual resolves by way of compromise.

Anna Freud suggests obsessive traits and uncontrollable impulsivity begin to develop if the ego maturation is premature or if there is slower development of drives. This contrasts with uncontrollable impulsivity that occurs when ego development lags behind drive development. This can also occur when, for constitutional reasons, ego strength is minimal and the given drive increases. These ego-factors impinge on the harmonious, simultaneous evolution of ego and drives. An imbalance in either one can create internal conflict.

Applying this theory to child sexual abuse, we believe the sexual abuse disrupts the evolution of equal development of drives and ego. That is, the drive component (sex and aggression) is being stimulated beyond ego development. Furthermore, the abuser accomplishes this disruption through intimidation and through distortion of reality and the child's sense of right and wrong. In addition, the physical approaches enforce irregular patterns of inhibition and disinhibition, rather than the child's normal rhythmic response in usual drive development. To deal with this externally provoked disruption of internal harmony, the child must invoke a life-saving mechanism to survive psychologically. This mechanism is *dissociation*.

Dissociation from the sexual abuse appears to be a prime and immediate method used by children to survive sexual assault during the abuse phase. Survival behaviors manifested by child victims during sexual assault include complying; negotiating; fighting; experiencing amnesia; crying; freezing in terror; and actively pretending to be somewhere or someone else. We define dissociation as a general process in which the mind fragments psychic integrity in the service of survival. In other words, the child victim diverts mental attention away from the abuse. Dissociation is a normal reaction to an emotionally loaded situation.

In order to understand dissociation, we need to discuss the role of ego and self-preservation. Self-preservation is vital to dissociation. Such self-preservation is an ego task, and external events that threaten people psychologically as well as physically call for this ego function. Because of extensive research, we understand this phenomenon clearly with adult victims of rape, combat, concentration camps, and hostage situation. However, less clear is the ego's role in child sexual abuse where the variable of violence is culturally defined. Conte (1984) suggests that our culturally bound definition of violence is too narrow and sexually biased in favor of men by not taking into account the psychological violence and force men use against women and children. Every time an adult sexually abuses a child, coercion, manipulation, force and violence are involved. To regard people who abuse children as nonviolent, argues Conte, is to fail to see them as their victims see them—as big and powerful.

The Role of Self-Preservation

Although no research exists regarding self-preservation and ego development in situations of child sexual abuse, we add this component to our model as an underlying assumption. In areas other than child sexual abuse, theorists have contributed to our understanding of the role of the ego in self-preservation. Hartmann's (1948) belief about the central role of the ego in relation to survival provides a basis for understanding the victim's capacity for self-care and self-protection.

Other contributors to the connection between ego and self-preservation include Glover (1933), Lowenstein (1949), Zetzel (1949), Rochlin (1965), and Mahler (1968). Kohut (1971) touches on the implications of self-preservation in the development of ego, especially in personality styles. The relationship between self-care and self-regulation is addressed by Sifneos and colleagues (1977); victim studies by Krystal and Raskin (1970) and Krystal (1977) discuss developmental disturbances and traumatic regressed states in substance abusers, concentration camp survivors, and sufferers of psychosomatic illness. These studies relate to ego survival during various levels of experience.

Khantzian and Mack (1983) examined self-preservation and self-care in drug abusers and summarize key points regarding these functions. They observe self-care to be a complete phenomenon involving multiple affective and cognitive processes, component functions, mechanisms of defense, and ego functions. The self-care function becomes internalized, primarily through the behaviors of the caretakers of the child. Their study (Khantzian and Mack, 1983) suggests that self-care capacities are closely associated with positive self-esteem and that a developing child needs to internalize the conviction, before self-care can begin, that he or she has value and is worth protecting. The need for protection by the child during sexual victimization suggests a comparison to the Khantzian and Mack study in that an adult forces a sexual act on a child, no adult protects the child and the child is unable to protect him or herself.

Splitting

Dissociation has the capacity to invoke the psychic mechanism of *splitting*, particularly if the repeated nature of child sexual abuse further burdens the child's psychic structure. Splitting is defined as a conflict between the demand of the instinct and the command of reality. The conflict persists as the center-point of a split in the ego; the rift never heals, but instead increases with time (Freud, 1938). Two indicators that splitting has occurred for the child victim are *ego-fragmentation* and *drive-disharmony*.

Ego-fragmentation can be observed through the victim's cognitions, self-representation, and body state. There is a split in trust and in adult protection. There is a disruption of body-comforting states as well as of self-care, self-preservation, and protective function. The victim may also exhibit a diffuse sense of right and wrong, a misplaced loyalty, and a justification for violence, pain, or intimidation. The child may also take on a self-depracatory pattern (e.g., "I'm to blame," "I'm no good; that is why this is happening," "I deserve this because I have feelings," "I'm responsible for what will happen to others in my family if I tell"). This may be accompanied by a distorted sense of causality; or a distorted sense of self, of others, or of personal rights.

Drive disharmony, or the split in drive function (sexual and aggressive drives) is noted through dissonant levels of stimulation and inhibition. That is, drive disharmony is evidenced through confused body integrity (arousal stimulation), through disruption in an evenly patterned expression of sexuality (symptoms include hyper-sexuality and repeated sexual rubbing of body), and through sexualized relationships.

Patterned Responses to Events

The child adjusts to the sexual abuse through the use of defense mechanisms and certain behavior patterns. Four such patterns that have been noted in children (Burgess et al., 1984) are presented below.

In the *avoidant pattern*, the child's anxiety about the abuse remains sealed off, either consciously or unconsciously. When asked about the event, the child denies it, refuses to recognize its occurrence, and may not be able to give a clear picture of it. The child often has a stoic demeanor and actively avoids discussion. The child is afraid of the offender. Also, the child tends to be oriented to the present; when not under stress, the child manages life as if nothing has happened.

The *stress pattern* may bring forth such symptoms as depression and self-destructive behavior. Relationships with peers may be terminated, family relationships may be strained, school difficulties may persist, and minor antisocial acts may surface. The child does not have a clear sense of right and wrong. The child refuses to talk about the event. Unconsciously the child feels responsible and "bad" and feels that he or she has injured both self and family.

In the *symptomatic pattern*, acute symptoms become chronic. The symptoms may be related to the event, or they may be a compound reaction to continued victimization or other traumatic events. There may be a cumulative reaction to additional stressful events, such as separation of parents or the death of a family member. The child's anxiety over being powerless is increased, and the child is unable to master and exert control over this anxiety.

When asked about the event, child victims in this pattern become quite anxious. They feel guilty and blame themselves—not the adult offender—for participating in the activity. These children are not in control of thoughts about the event; the event is still operant and conscious. Family relationships are often unstable, peer relationships may not be re-established, and the victims are not successful in socializing with children of the same age and may associate with younger children. They may drop out of school, continue sexually explicit behaviors, and be victimized again. They believe they should have known better and they should have told their parents. In addition, they are oriented to the past and may be hopeless about the future, believing it impossible to make up for what happened.

In the *pattern of identification with the abuser*, the child has introjected some characteristics of the anxiety caused by the abuse and has assimilated the anxiety by impersonating the aggressor. The child transforms himself or herself from the person threatened into the person who makes the threat. The child masters anxiety by exploiting others and by adopting an antisocial position toward peers, school, and family.

In talking about the event, the child who identifies with the abuser minimizes the exploitation, resents the interference of the authorities, and feels there is "much ado about nothing." The child maintains emotional, social, and economic ties with the offender and feels sorry or angry that the adult was exposed. This child has difficulties with authorities, especially in school. Use of drugs and alcohol, which is often part of the sexual abuse, continues and increases. There is a shift in the child's belief system that supports the antisocial behavior.

It is in the *psychotic pattern* that the most profound symptoms are noted. The child is unable to distinguish reality; the ego boundaries are significantly blurred. Primary symptoms may herald the secondary (psychotic) symptoms, such as loose associations prior to the shattering of cognitive, emotional, and physiological integration of the child. There is marked restricted ego development, and the traumatic event is split off and buried in delusional symptoms and material. There is splitting noted in interpersonal relationships, regressive behavior, and primitive, fixed, sexualized thinking patterns. For example, the child may report seeing the face of the abuser everywhere he or she goes.

FRAMEWORK UTILIZATION

Our cognitive-behavioral conceptual framework for examining traumatic event processing in sexual abuse victims is an initial model for understanding the child-victim experience. It is important to keep in mind limitations associated with its use. First, using this model does not allow direct observation of the victim's cognitive processes. We are neither present at the time of the events nor are there adequate devices for direct measurement of cognitive processes.

Second, the interval between victimization and development of complete response patterns allows other variables, such as time, life stresses, and events, to intervene. Research using this model cannot control for these intervening factors.

Third, the psychodynamic concepts of ego fragmentation and drive disharmony are abstract phenomena. Thus they are subject to the above limitations imposed by intervening factors.

Given these limitations, we suggest this framework as a way to begin to understand the structure of the victim experience for the child and as a guide for the therapist in exploring the meaning of the event for all family members.

REFERENCES

Browne, A. & Finkelhor, D. (1984). *The Impact of Child Sexual Abuse.* Unpublished paper, University of New Hampshire, Durham, N.H.

Burgess, A.W., Hartman, C.R., McCausland, M.P. & Powers, P. (1984). Response patterns in children and adolescents exploited through sex rings and pornography. *American Journal of Psychiatry, 141* (5) 656–662.

Conte, J.R. (1984). Progress in treating the sexual abuse of children. *Social Work,* May–June, 258–263.

Egendorf, A., Kadushin, C., Laufer, R., et al., (1981). *Legacies of Vietnam.* Washington, D.C.: U.S. Government Printing Office.

Erikson, E. (1952). *Childhood and Society,* New York: Norton Co.

Figley, C.R. (1978). *Stress Disorders Among Vietnam Veterans: Theory, Research and Treatment.* New York: Brunner/Mazel Publ.

Freud, A. (1983). Problems of Pathogenesis. In *The Psychoanalytic Study of the Child 38* (Eds.) A.J. Solnit, R.S. Eissler & P.B. Neubauer. New Haven: Yale University Press.

Glover, E. (1933). The relation of perversion formation to the development of reality sense. *International Journal of Psychoanalysis, 14,* 486–504.

Hartmann, H. (1948). Comments on the psychoanalytic theory of instinctual drives. In *Essays on Ego Psychology.* New York: Int. Univ. Press, 69–89.

Horowitz, M.J. (1976). *Stress Response Syndrcme.* New York: Jason Aronson, Inc.

Khantzian, E.J. and Mack, J.E. (1983). Self-preservation and the care of the self: Ego instincts reconsidered. *The Psychoanalytic Study of the Child 38* (Eds) A.J. Solnit, R.S. Eissler & P.B. Neubauer. New Haven: Yale University Press.

Kohut, H. (1971). *The Analysis of Self.* New York: International University Press.

Lowenstein, R.M. (1949). The vital or somatic instincts. *International Journal of Psychoanalysis, 21,* 377–400.

Krystal, H. (1977). Self-representation and the capacity for self-care. *Annu. Psychoanal. 6:*209–246.

Krystal, H. & Raskin, H.A. (1970). *Drug Dependence.* Detroit: Wayne State University Press.

Mahler, M.S. (1968). *On Human Symbiosis and the Vicissitudes of Individuation.* New York: International Universities Press.

Rochlin, G. (1965). *Griefs and Discontents.* Boston: Little, Brown & Co.

Sifneos, P., Apfel-Savitz, R. & Frankl, F. (1977). The phenomenon of 'alexethymia.' *Psychother. Psychosom. 28:*47–57.

Zetzel, E.R. (1949). Anxiety and the capacity to bear it. *International Journal of Psychoanalysis, 30,* 1–12.

The Apology Session

Terry S. Trepper

A number of programs for the treatment of intrafamily child sexual abuse have been described recently (e.g., Anderson and Schaffer, 1979; Giaretto, 1981, 1982; Justice and Justice, 1979). Although this is an encouraging beginning, a need exists for specific techniques to be presented which may prove useful to therapists working with incest families. The purpose of this paper is to describe one technique which we have found extremely useful in the family treatment of incest, the *apology session*.

Variations of the apology session technique have been presented elsewhere. For example, Justice and Justice (1979) during their first family interview may ask the parents to apologize to the daughter for the abuse. James and Nasjleti (1983) describe a *confrontation* session which permits the daughter to openly confront her parents about the abuse and her feelings toward them. The intervention described here, however, differs significantly in both the purpose and format of these other techniques.

Before describing the apology session itself, it may be helpful to briefly outline the treatment program upon which it is based (for a complete description of a systemically based family treatment program for intrafamily sexual abuse, see Barrett et al.).

TREATMENT PROGRAM

Although a number of programs exist for the treatment of intrafamily child sexual abuse, ours is one of the few to be based primarily on systemic family therapy. As such, ours involves the entire family in the assessment, treatment, and follow-up phases of therapy.

Underlying Assumptions

There are a number of assumptions underlying this model. First, there are multiple reasons for the presence of incestuous behavior in a family,

Terry S. Trepper is the Director of the Family Studies Center and Associate Professor of Psychology at Purdue University Calumet. He also has a private practice in Chicago.

but in most cases the family structure plays an extremely important role in contributing and maintaining the problem. Second, therapy must include a programmatic component that addresses the *restructuring* of the family system. Restructuring refers to altering the inappropriate cross-generational coalitions, dysfunctional power hierarchies, and problem-engendering interactional behavior patterns. Third, although we view the abusing parent as ultimately responsible for the inappropriate sexual behavior, each family member has an important role to play in the family's ability to improve. That is, our goal is to change the family's structure and functioning so that the likelihood of future abuse is lessened.

Finally, it is our strong conviction that it is in the best interest of the family to remain together during the course of therapy rather than receive separate treatment. This, of course, will depend on the wishes of the family, the desires of the child victim, and the view of the therapist as to the "treatability" of the family. However, we feel there is potentially less trauma and a better chance for change when all are involved with the therapy.

Program Format

The program begins with a formal assessment period, usually 4–6 weeks, where the individuals, the family system, and the family's external systems are evaluated. In this evaluation we determine which factors contributes to the family's vulnerability to incest, which precipitating events or situations typically precede an abusive episode, and what coping mechanisms the family utilizes (or lacks). Once the family is admitted to the program (i.e., is determined to be amenable to treatment), we begin formal therapy sessions. These may include whole family, dyadic, individual, and group sessions. The program orientation is generally structural-strategic, but we try to include a variety of interventions from the insight-working through, behavioral, modeling, and strategic-paradoxical frameworks (Feldman, 1976).

APOLOGY SESSION

One major intervention with which we usually begin is the *apology session*. This is actually a therapeutic ritual which involves many weeks of planning and preparation on the part of the family, and which has proven to have a profound impact on the course of the therapy. We have found that ritualizing the apology session, making it an "event" or milestone for the family, has made it both a useful structural intervention for that session and a point to which all future interventions are referred.

Pre-Apology Sessions

Once the family is accepted into the program, we begin to work immediately with the parents for the next several sessions. We call these the "pre-apology sessions," whose purpose is to coach the parents on presenting the formal apology. Since this will require both parents accepting a portion of the responsibility for the current problems of the family, we work to help them accept that responsibility which is theirs both as individuals and as parents.

Often one parent wishes to focus the blame on the other; for example, from the mother, "It's all his fault . . . I mean, he's the one who did it!''; or from the father, "If she had just been there sexually for me, I would never have had to go to my daughter,'' or from either, "If our daughter had not been so seductive (available, unable to tell someone, etc.) this would have never happened!''

More commonly, however, one parent wishes to take all of the blame or responsibility for what has occurred. We try to guide them into accepting that which is theirs individually. For example, we will work with the father to accept the ultimate responsibility for the incest itself. We may work with the mother to accept some responsibility for not believing her daughter if she were told. We also work with them both to accept that responsibility which is theirs as parents, for example by not dealing with their marital or sexual problems through more appropriate means.

During this time we have concurrent sessions with the abused child to prepare her for the apology session. Although we do not specifically describe the session, we make a determination whether or not she is ready, or if there are any signals that this type of session will do any harm. We typically will ask directly, "How would you feel if your parents apologized to you, formally and publicly, and promised to make things different from now on?" Of particular concern is whether she displays a great amount of anger at either parent or a strong sense that a session such as this will "let them off the hook." Also of concern is if she thinks somehow a session like this might precipitate further abuse. It should be noted that only a few times has a child *not* wished to have the apology session. In general, they too see this as an important first step in changing the family.

Apology Session Format

The next step is the actual apology session. The entire family is present for this meeting, and with their permission we videotape the proceedings for use with them at a later date. The arrangement of the room is critical, with the parents sitting together facing the children, and the therapist sitting beside the parents. We want a seating arrangement that symbolizes the new structure of the family; that is, the parents *together* and the children functioning in the same generation.

The parents begin the session by explaining to the children why they are all here today, summarizing the reasons for the family having the trouble it is having, and, if anyone does not know about the incest, explaining about the abuse in a way the children can understand. It is critical for even the youngest children in a family to know what specifically is the reason the family is currently not all living together, and why people are angry with one another. It is our experience that if the younger non-abused children are not told (and unfortunately sometimes even when they are) they think they are in some way to blame. The parents are coached in the pre-apology sessions on ways they may tell the unaware children, but we always do insist that the entire family be told. There can be no more secrets in this family.

During the session, both parents state what they apologize to the family for, and accept a portion of the responsibility. They then explain what they will do to make the situation better, and what they would like from the children. The children are encouraged to ask any questions they have about the incident, or the future of their families. They are then asked to consider what it will mean to accept their parents' apology. It does *not* imply the children can not be angry with their parents, nor even necessarily feel safe with them at the present. It does mean, however, that they will allow their parents the chance to make their family better, and that they will work with the parents in therapy to correct the problems which contributed to the abuse.

The therapist's role during the session is to coach the parents and children, clarify what is being said, and keep the process on track. To accomplish this, the therapist moves around to sit by the person speaking, and is supportive and encouraging. At the end of the session, the family is told that this was a milestone in their life, that although therapy will be difficult at times, the worst is over and they are now free to move forward as a family. We feel this optimism portrayed by the therapist is the family's reward for all they have been through up until now. It is indeed upward from here on end.

A SAMPLE APOLOGY SESSION

The following is an edited transcript of an actual apology session. The Smith family (not their real names) was referred by Protective Services after it was discovered that the two oldest daughters, Betty, 17, and Barb, 16, had been sexually abused by their natural father during the previous two years, the most recent being during a short hospital stay by the mother. There are three younger children, a boy, 13, a girl, 10, and a boy, 5. None of the other children were abused. The three girls were placed in a foster home, which is the focus of crisis for the family at this time.

The mother was involved sexually with her father during her early adolescence, although this was denied to the therapist until a few months after this interview. This may explain her suspicion of incest alluded to during this session. At this point, the parents see the father's alcohol abuse as the primary cause of the incest. They will expand this notion during the next few months into a more complete understanding of their family's dynamics which made them vulnerable to sexual abuse. The family had five weeks of assessment sessions, and the parents had two sessions of "pre-apology" planning. The entire family was present for this session.

Father: We had a bad situation happen while mom was in the hospital, when dad and Barb got involved in a sexual affair, you know, and that's what brought all this about. And I know you're embarrassed but there's no sense in being embarrassed. You shouldn't be embarrassed in front of us, there's no sense being embarrassed in front of Dr. Trepper. They're here to help us see why it happened and different ways of avoiding situations like that in the future. And that's the reason you were taken from the home. Everybody realizes that. We're here today to, well, since that situation happened we kind of got back together a little bit with our feelings and our actions and this and that and the other. And I'm apologizing to you Barb, and you two girls and for me being the cause of you being removed from the home. This today is to apologize publicly before strangers so that other people can hear this and see that we apologized and maybe that we mean what we said and not just a bunch of lip action to kind of get off light. It was pointed out to me that, I guess if they didn't have this program I would have gone to jail for this. And Lord knows that you guys might have been returned to mom and might not have. I don't really know that. But they have the benefit of this program here and we're taking advantage of this program to pull us back together as a family. And I think we have got a lot a good qualities as a family except for that business about getting drunk and letting sex enter my life where it has no business. I mean my sex is my sex and your sex is your sex but together, that it's not right. And even though I'm older, and I'm more responsible because I'm older, you have a responsibility, too, not to enter into those type of things. It's just as easy to go to mom and say, "Well dad tried to feel me up today" or "Dad tried this or dad tried that," and let mom make an attempt to help. And if mom doesn't make an attempt to help then you can reach out outside the family to somebody else like Aunt _____ or Uncle _____ or maybe some friend of yours. (To mother) So uh, are you gonna say anything?

Mother: Well um . . . I feel bad about what happened and everybody knows it but. . . .

Therapist: I want to tell you that. . . .

Mother: I want to tell you that I'm sorry you're out of our house. I wish there could have been another way but I'm glad it happened because a lot of things have been brought out. I'm not afraid anymore . . . (crying) and I know you kids don't have to be afraid anymore and that's so important to me and I know dad is trying not to drink anymore. I can't promise you it'll never happen again because I don't know. . . .

Therapist: What can you promise?

Mother: I can promise you that if anything like this ever does happen again, that you can come to tell me and I know where to go to get help. I think if it ever happened again we know where to go and we know where to come to for the help. Before I feared that dad would go to jail and it's kinda hard to explain when you love somebody that you don't want them to go to jail but it's also hard to explain that you don't want your little girls hurt anymore.

Therapist: So what can you promise the girls?

Mother: I can promise you that if anything like this ever happens again that I will come here and I'll find help for us. It doesn't have to happen again. You can come and tell me, you don't have to be afraid of Dad no more because there's nothing dad's gonna do to hurt you. I guess I'm glad it happened. . . . It's just as much my fault as it is his because I knew there was a possibility that it could be happening. I think both you big girls know that. I mean, nights I sat up in the living room and waited for him to pass out so I could go to sleep so that I knew nothing would happen. In the back of my mind I knew that it was possible that it could happen. I'm telling you both that if anything like this ever happens, to come to me and tell me, to scream out, scream your lungs out from the basement, if you have to. But don't let it happen. Alright, this was one time I wasn't there, ok. You couldn't scream out to me, I was quite far away from you but I'm sorry that this happened. I'm sorry that you have to be away from our home. But this is my apology right here.

Father: (interrupting) Mom's got everyone down in the dumps. Now it's serious, what she's saying but the point mom's trying to bring out is. . . .

Therapist: It's important that you speak for yourself. . . . Sometimes you have a tendency to speak for others in the family.

Father: I know . . . (laughing) I know. . . .

Therapist: So what can *you* promise?

Father: (To the children) I promise you it will not happen again and I'm telling you in front of your mother, your brothers, your sisters, Dr. Trepper, that all you have to do is go to your mother and you will get instantaneous help. You won't have to wait for her to come here as she says. She'll take care of it on the spot. But there won't be any need for that, but if there is, that's a little guarantee that you got, that you can do something about the problem.

It should be noted that some of the tentativeness in the parents' presentation reflects their concurrent involvement with Alcoholics Anonymous and ALANON. One of the AA tenets is "One Day at a Time," and that they are therefore caught in the bind of being asked to make a promise while also being told not to make any promises. Our way of dealing with this common dilemma is to simply ignore the obvious contradiction and instead respond to the underlying meaning, in this case "I am going to try my best not to let it happen again."

After this the children were asked for their reactions. Each was given a turn to say anything, good or bad, about what the parents had said. In this session, as in most where the incest was not associated with violence or physical abuse, the children said they accepted their parents' apology, were not afraid of it happening again, and understood what they are supposed to do if it did. The parents were then asked to tell the children what apologizing to them was like.

Characteristically, father answered first:

Father: If you think this is easy, you ought to be sitting here in my boots to have to say something in front of Dr. Trepper and your mother. I've apologized for it and I'm getting help for it. I've stopped drinking for it. I go to meetings four times a week for it. We go to family sessions, I come to see Dr. Trepper once a week, and God only knows what kind of hoops he's gonna have me jumping through, and I apologize that it is gonna absolutely be the end of it as far as I'm concerned. I promise it'll never happen again to the best of my ability and I can't do anything more than apologize to you and see that it doesn't happen again.

Therapist: And for you?

Mother: This has been hard, very hard . . . but I'm glad to get to tell them, and I'm glad they accept our apology. That's very important to us.

We have coached the parents on what they should now expect from the children once the apology session is complete. We are concerned that the children do not use the incest or their parents' apology as a means of gaining power. This could prove as dysfunctional as the father's misused power while the abuse was occurring.

Therapist: What do you want to tell the children about what you two expect from them?

Father: In the future, I don't want to hear any of you saying "Oh, I don't have to clean my room after what you did to me,'' or ''I can go out with anybody I want, since you did so and so to me.'' Just cause I screwed up doesn't mean that I'm not your father and she's not your mother and that we don't have a right to do what we think is best for you . . . that's why we're apologizing. That's all out. This subject will be closed right here and now. We finish this thing except for getting help on how not for this to happen again.

Therapist: Does this mean if they have some concerns, they couldn't come to you? That they can't talk about the incest or their feelings or fears about it?

Father: Oh no, no, no. I mean you can come to me. If there's anything that comes up that they want to talk over with me or their mother, fine. Bring it right out in the open. But what I mean is don't be whining for a present and say, well dad, you remember when mom was in the hospital and twist my arm so that you won't say anything about that. From that stand point it's closed. But if you've got some feelings or maybe boyfriend troubles or whatever, you know what I mean, uh, you want to feel free to come to your mother or your father. Now I think you will. I think naturally, probably I'm not getting that point across too well, but I think they know. . . .

Therapist: You're doing fine.

Father: I hope they get the message, you know what I mean.

Therapist: Why don't you ask them?

When he did, each one responded that they understood. The therapist again reminded the children that they were encouraged to talk as much as they wanted about their feelings concerning the incest, including anger feelings. Mother also reiterated that point.

The last part of the session focused on what the children's responsibility is in making the family better. Although the purpose of the apology session is to allow the parents to present a ''new beginning,'' it is equally important that the children see that they as family members have much to do with the future success of the family.

Therapist: Do you have anything to add to in terms of what you think the children's responsibility is now?

Mother: Oh, I just, I think that it's their responsibility to come to us and say, ''Hey, it's happening again.'' You know, we're guilty of what we did, but we're getting help for it. It's over with, it stops right here, you know. Nobody's gonna pass the buck any further than this. We're right here in this session, and we're gonna get help for what happened.

Therapist: You sound very firm, very firm.

Mother: I am.

Therapist: Very firm in that "I am guilty of what occurred. I am responsible and I will protect you."

Mother: I will, I will protect them. That's the most important thing I can tell them.

CONCLUSIONS

There are a number of elements that are crucial for the success of this intervention. First, it is essential that the parents' apology be genuine. This may not mean that at this time in therapy they completely accept their own responsibility. It must mean, however, that they genuinely are sorry for that piece which was theirs, and that they genuinely want it not to happen again. Second, it is important that the parents give the children the clear message that the problem is both parents' responsibilities. They should demonstrate a marital and parental cohesiveness to the children. Third, the session should remain focused on the apology, the responsibilities of each family member to make things better, and the promise of better things to come. Other issues and concerns should be left for later sessions.

The apology session can be a useful early-stage intervention to quickly and dramatically institute change in the sexually abusing family. Although there are some families with whom this intervention may not be appropriate, in most cases it can provide the symbolic turning point from which meaningful family change may occur.

REFERENCES

Anderson, L. M., and Shafer, G. (1979). The character-disordered family: A community treatment model for family sexual abuse. *American Journal of Orthopsychiatry*, 49, 436–445.

Feldman, L. (1976). Strategies and techniques of family therapy. *American Journal of Psychotherapy*, 30, 14–28.

Giaretto, H. (1981). A comprehensive child sexual abuse treatment program. *Child Abuse and Neglect*, 6, 263–278.

Giaretto, H. (1982). *Integrated Treatment of Child Sexual Abuse*, Palo Alto, CA: Science and Behavior Books.

James, B., and Nasjleti, M. (1983). *Treating Sexually Abused Children and their Families.* Palo Alto, CA: Consulting Psychologists Press.

Justice, B., and Justice, R. (1979). *The Broken Taboo.* New York: Human Sciences Press.

Court Testimony in Cases
of Intrafamily Child Sexual Abuse:
A Practical Guide
for the Family Therapist

Stephen Schweitzer
Robert T. Kurlychek

Despite criticisms and cautions (e.g., Ennis & Litwack, 1974; Goldzband, 1982; Wells, 1983) mental health professionals are becoming more involved in the legal process. A significant number of psychologists and psychiatrists regularly appear in court as expert witnesses and are generally well prepared for their foray into the adversarial process. However, regardless of educational level, for family therapists who come to court because they were involved in a treatment situation that later ended up in litigation, offering courtroom testimony can be frightening and bewildering if unprepared. It is to these uninitiated first-timers that this paper is directed.

Because the problem of intrafamily sexuality is being acknowledged and reported more, it is not surprising that family therapists are becoming more involved in the assessment and treatment process. Because of the legal implication of this problem, the probability that a therapist will become involved in the legal process is increasing. A healthy discomfort at entering this foreign territory is natural and even helpful in motivating the responsible professional to become adequately prepared.

The purpose of this paper is to provide the family therapist with specific information and suggestions for adequately preparing for that time when he or she may have to testify in court in cases of intrafamily child sexual abuse. We will focus on the ways in which a family therapist may become involved in the legal process, describe some basic legal terms and concepts relevant to these cases, and offer a family therapist's "primer" for giving court testimony.

Stephen Schweitzer, Ph.D., is Associate Professor of Counseling Psychology at the University of Oregon, and Robert T. Kurlychek, Ph.D., is with Sacred Heart Medical Center, Eugene, Oregon.

A WIDE VARIETY OF POSSIBLE INVOLVEMENTS

Surprisingly, a family therapist may be involved in the judicial process for a large number of reasons and at various junctures in the process. The therapist may be currently evaluating or treating a family where inappropriate sexual behavior is revealed. He or she might be asked to treat an offender and family as part of a probationary decree. Oftentimes therapists are called upon to serve as a consultant in preparing a case, by the prosecutor or defendant in a criminal case, or by either side in a civil litigation. With more attention being paid to sexual abuse, some women who were victimized as children are initiating civil law suits years later (Hyde & Kaufman, 1984). Conceivably a therapist who treated or who is treating such an individual may be called to testify.

Because some of the principal figures in the legal process are often very young, the issue of credibility of children witnesses is raised (Marin, Holmes, Guth, & Kovac, 1979). It is not unusual for a child to change his testimony in court and deny that abuse has occurred, because of threat, shame, or fear of rejection by one or more family members. Naturally, defense attorneys will try to discredit the child, who is often the only witness. (This is known as "impeaching the witness".) A therapist experienced in working with children or who has evaluated and/or treated the child in question may be asked to express an opinion regarding probable credibility. The permissibility of expert testimony regarding this aspect of the "sexually abused child syndrome" differs from state to state (Wells, 1983). In a 1983 landmark case, State v. Middleton, the Oregon Supreme Court upheld this use of expert testimony, known as "rehabilitating the witness". For any credibility problems, it is important to make the jury aware that reluctance or inconsistency in the face of cross-examination is often a typical reaction of child victims, and this case should be cited (294 Or. 427, 657 P. 2d 1215 (1983)).

The therapist can also contribute by assisting in the preparation of a sexually abused child and/or other family members for court testimony (Bauer, 1983). Role-playing is especially effective in accomplishing this. Providing support for the child before, during, and/or after the often long, emotionally exhausting legal process is another important service provided by the therapist. The child's feelings can range from anxiety and fright to self-doubt to relief. Some post-trial therapy should always be provided.

BASIC LEGAL TERMS AND CONCEPTS

A *material witness* can only testify to firsthand observations. The clinician may be asked to state that a child described sexual activity to you. Reporting *hearsay* (i.e., information not directly witnessed by you) or stating opinions is not permitted. More latitude is given to the *expert witness* who can discuss any information or evidence used (directly observed or not) in arriving at his or her opinion. Of course, it is of basic importance to find out prior to testimony how you are being viewed by the attorney who is calling you to testify. In general, the more credentials one has (e.g., psychiatrist, licensed psychologist), the more likely he or she will be considered an expert witness, although experience also carries important weight, and social workers are often called as expert witnesses (see "Your Qualifications" below).

A *subpoena* is a document requested by an attorney and issued by the court clerk requiring an individual to appear at a certain time, date, and place for the purpose of giving sworn testimony. It is important to contact the issuing attorney immediately, especially if there is a scheduling conflict. Generally, alternate arrangements can be made. Not to appear at the given time without proper excuse can be considered contempt of court and penalties can be imposed. A person can be subpoenaed by the state, the parents' attorney, or the child's attorney (*guardian ad litem*). If the subpoena has *duces tecum* printed on it, then you are required to produce all records pertaining to the client. Thus, it becomes important to read the subpoena carefully to avoid producing too little to too much information.

The *trier of fact* is the decision-making agent. In most criminal cases of child abuse, this is the jury. If jury privilege is waved (sometimes done for tactical reasons) the responsibility is shifted to the judge. An opposing attorney may exercise his or her right to *discovery*: (i.e., to know what evidence will be introduced before a trial or hearing) by asking for a *deposition*. This generally involves attorneys from each side, a court reporter who records the proceedings (it may also be videotaped), and the therapist being "deposed". This process often takes place in an attorney's office or even at the therapist's office. Do not be fooled by the informality of the situation. One must be as prepared and as on guard as if it were taking place in court. This information can be brought out in court and the clinician's credibility questioned if there is any change in your statements.

Incest is generally defined as "a sexual relationship between people of kinship pattern for whom marriage is prohibited by law" (Fraser, 1981). The legal definitions are more complex and may differ from state to state. There are three types of child sexual abuse: non-touching, touching, and violent touching (Fraser, 1981). Criminal sexual abuse is thus differentially defined within each state on the basis of the child's age, length of time of abuse, type of abuse, and damage or trauma suffered by the child. Non-touching acts include exhibitionism, voyeurism, exposure to adult sexual activity, obscene phone calls, and verbal sexual abuse. Touching acts include anal and vaginal intercourse, oral sex, masturbation, and fondling. Violent touching acts involve serious bodily injury or threat of injury (rape) along with the aforementioned acts. The majority of intrafamily sexual abuse cases involve non-violent touching acts. States often differentiate sexual activities with children under 14 versus those with children between 14 and 18 (the age of emancipation).

Most states have multiple laws which apply to these cases. Criminal law defines deviant sexual behavior (including incest and sodomy) and the prosecution of alleged offenders takes place in criminal court. Civil law includes child protection statutes which provide for the intervention by state agencies and the possible removal of the child from the home. Such decisions are made in juvenile or civil court. The therapist may find himself in any of four types of hearing, two within each system.

In juvenile court, the first major hearing is the *adjudicatory hearing*, which attempts to resolve the question of whether sexual abuse as defined by state law has taken place. If not proven, all legal proceedings cease; otherwise, a *dispositional hearing* is held to decide on child custody and treatment for the victim. In criminal court, a *preliminary hearing* is first held in which the district attorney attempts to present sufficient evidence that sexual abuse has been committed. (This is sometimes done before a grand jury and is sometimes skipped completely.) The final criminal proceeding is the *trial*, where a guilty verdict or plea can result in a fine, jail sentence, or both. Sentences are sometimes deferred while the perpetrator undergoes rehabilitative therapy.

A THERAPIST'S PRIMER FOR COURT TESTIMONY

Preparing for the Legal Process

The most beneficial time to prepare for court testimony is not after the subpoena arrives but by taking steps to become the most responsible, professional, and ethical family therapist one can be on a day-to-day, case-by-case basis. In other words, if therapists organize their professional life according to the state-of-the-art in the field they will be about eighty-percent prepared for that potential day in court.

Review your record keeping and charting procedures; randomly select a case. Would you feel knowledgeable and comfortable explaining your assessment, decisions, and interventions to others? Attempt to treat every case as if it might eventually wind up in court, because it might! Careful recording of observations of family interactions is especially important.

An agency or clinic can establish a resource center that can be generally informative and educative when a specific case arises. A number of books and articles have been published to assist mental health professionals involved in the general legal process (e.g., Bartol, 1983; Blau, 1984; Brodsky, 1977; Kurlychek & DeHeer, 1982; Shapiro, 1984) while others are more specific to family therapy issues (Derdeyn, 1975; Goldzband, 1982; Litwack, Garber, & Fenster, 1979; Nichols, 1980; Woody, 1977) and child sexual abuse issues (Sgroi, 1982; Mrazek & Kempe, 1981). It also can be very helpful to become familiar with works designed to prepare attorneys to effectively deal with mental health witnesses (e.g., Goulett, 1965; Ziskin, 1981a, 1981b) because sooner or later you may be faced with some of their discrediting tactics. Pre-testimony preparation can be aided by consultation with mental health colleagues who have testified in similar situations in your community. It may also be helpful to observe an experienced psychiatrist or psychologist providing testimony (Kurlychek & DeHeer, 1982).

The importance of being professionally informed and adequately trained in your area of practice cannot be stressed enough. Unfortunately, while the majority of community mental health centers consider intrafamily sexual abuse to be their primary sex-related problem, counselors are often inadequately trained to deal with these cases and widespread "myths" abound in this area (Trepper & Traicoff, 1983). It is important to keep up with relevant literature and seek continuing education experiences. Be aware of the existence of beliefs and classification systems other than your own or those supported by your agency (cf. Alford, Kasper, & Baumann, 1984; Trepper & Traicoff, 1983). We recommend to therapists that they familiarize themselves with a questionnaire developed by Johnson and Blazer (1980) to assess knowledge in the area of sex offenses.

It is essential to know your current state laws regarding the reporting of child abuse and how it applies to your professional classification. Surprisingly, many mental health professionals are unaware of or ignore these laws (Swoboda, Elwork, Sales & Levine, 1978). Various regulations with regard to privileged communication may apply for different classifications of professionals in the mental health field. For example, a licensed psychologist may be exempt from the requirement to report abuse by a state statute while a mental health agency counselor is not. Be aware of the guidelines of confidentiality at the outset of the relationship. The "privilege" of confidentiality normally belongs to the client in a counselor-client relationship. However, in cases of intrafamily sexual abuse, the laws override the privilege and the judge can require you to reveal confidentially-obtained material.

The Pretrial Conference

Whatever the circumstances leading to your involvement in the judicial process, it is imperative to discuss the eventual testimony with the attorney who initiated contact long before you are on the witness stand. Ideally this is done in person but may also be accomplished via the telephone. Since your reputation may be at stake, you must take responsibility for this conference. In preparing for the trial, collaboration with the attorney is in your best interest. It sometimes may be desirable to consult the opposing attorney and even the judge before the trial in an attempt to minimize the trauma for the victim. However, this should be done in concert with the attorney who called you.

It is important to learn of the attorney's overall goals and how you fit in. Oftentimes, what you see as being the central issue is not as important to the attorney. Learn the pertinent facts of the case. Seek to determine what questions he or she plans to ask you and what questions you might anticipate upon cross-examination. It is crucial to review all testimony with the attorney to insure that it is free of professional jargon and easily understood. Attempt to prepare for the expected cross-examination. Are there other mental health professionals testifying? If so, try to review his or her input in a fair and respectful manner. Remember that professional infighting can do both the client and the profession a disservice and may result in later retaliation.

This may be your first time in court but it also may be this attorney's first time questioning a professional witness in a case involving intrafamily sexual abuse. This is your area of expertise. Be prepared to be assertive and educate the attorney regarding theoretical and clinical issues in the area. The attorney will appreciate any relevant literature pertaining to your area of expertise, as well as anything you have previously published or presented.

It may be helpful to prepare a series of questions that the attorney can ask of you which will explain, step-by-step, concepts that you believe are critical to the case. Such concepts may include family dynamics, differentiating unmet emotional needs from seductive behavior, child developmental issues, and various aspects of the "sexually abused child syndrome". In the majority of cases of intrafamily sexual abuse, the following components of this syndrome may be brought to light. There is usually no proof of physical trauma or violence, (which is the hallmark of most other criminal assault prosecutions). The abuse probably progressed from touching to more serious transgressions like intercourse over a period of time, and persisted for years. Although children either sense or know that something is wrong, they sometimes enjoy the attention. They keep the activities secret because of guilt, fear, or family loyalty. There is usually a time delay between the last activity and ultimate disclosure. The family is usually dysfunctional in a number of other areas besides sexual abuse, such as a problematic marital relationship, ineffective or inadequate communication, and unclear intergenerational boundaries. There are also a number of individual personality characteristics of the perpetrator and the spouse which may contribute to intrafamily child sexual abuse.

Some Evaluation Issues

For the family therapist who is currently treating the family, providing what may be damaging testimony in court may preclude future work with the family. In such cases, it is best to suggest to the attorney that another professional be called in to evaluate the family. Agencies often use a team of mental health professionals, which may include psychiatrists, psychologists, social workers, counselors, and nurses, for evaluative purposes. Again, if there is a primary therapist, it is best if s/he is not called as witness.

A clear and concise diagnostic assessment should be jargon free and focused on test results, concrete behavioral descriptions and observations rather than conclusory statements which are the function of the judge and/or jury. The expert witness may offer an opinion, but should offer the facts upon which it is based. Family dynamics are best understood by observing the family. How do they interact? What are the parents' attitudes toward the child since the revelation of abuse? How does the child feel about these reactions? Have feelings and conflicts been dealt with openly and completely? Has the offender taken responsibility for his behavior? Pertinent family history (e.g., sexual abuse suffered by the perpetrator) is important and should be carefully obtained. Common behavioral indicators exhibited by victims include: depression, lethargy, isolation from peers, fear of men, running away, sleep disturbance or nightmares, acting-out, aggressive behaviors like bed-wetting, overly compliant behavior, seductive behavior, suicidal feelings, lack of trust, inability to concentrate at school or sudden drop in school performance, and persistent and inappropriate sexual play with self, toys, or peers.

Psychologists often administer a battery of developmental, cognitive, and projective tests. Examples of projective tests are the Kinetic Family Drawing test and the Conger Sentence Completion test. Common themes which emerge are unmet dependency needs, oral deprivation, and lack of nurturance (Johnston, 1976). The evaluator(s) should have knowledge of child development, abnormal child behaviors, adult psychopathology and family dynamics. Test accuracy and the child's credibility and competency should be determined by comparing responses to those of the average child and by noting consistency and spontaneity. Use the child's exact language, i.e., synonyms for sexual acts and body parts, when summarizing your findings and testifying.

Your Qualifications

When you are first called to the stand as an expert witness your attorney will attempt to have you "qualified" by the judge. Facts such as your educational and occupational background, professional accomplishments (including your publications, thesis, or dissertation), and court-related experience will be presented. You may be questioned about the current literature and state of knowledge regarding intrafamily sexual abuse, and the amount of time you spend in research or treatment in this area. It can be useful to have a comprehensive bibliography available for the court, as well as copies of pertinent literature. Questioning to qualify the family therapist as an expert witness may be quite extensive and complex. Upon your attorney's advice, you should be well prepared, much as you would for a licensing exam or dissertation defense. Here again, the pre-trial conference is the time to discuss how your qualifications will be presented. You should provide your attorney with a current resume of your professional and educational credentials.

If an opposing attorney wants to discredit you, he or she can always find something. The attorney is likely to focus on your education especially if you do not have an M.D. or Ph.D. They also may focus on the time period you have been practicing. While you may have worked with numerous abuse cases, you may be asked "How many families with two natural children and two stepchildren have you worked with (the specific case being addressed)? This may be your first time in court or your forty-first but someone can always say it's not enough.

Do not take such strategies personally and do not become intimidated. It can work both ways. If this is your first or second time in court be proud of it! Have your attorney emphasize that you are not a professional witness (read "hired gun"). You are a clinician working in the trenches. Even though you may not have a doctoral degree you may have years of experience dealing with family issues. The courts will usually honor this.

Advocacy vs Objectivity: The Trial or Hearing

The legal process is an adversarial one and the role of the attorney is to advocate for the client or for his or her point of view (e.g., criminal prosecution). It is important that the family therapist not get drawn into "taking sides". While this admonition is repeated often (e.g., Chamberlain, Krell, & Preis, 1982; MacDonald, 1969), pure objectivity is often not possible nor desirable. One can have an honest viewpoint or way of looking at a problem (bias) and be an advocate of this position in court. A therapist who is treating an incest family and believes in maintaining the family unit may be opposed by a worker from a children's services unit that has a firm policy of permanent removal of the victim from the home. The family therapist must become an "objective advocate" of his or her position and be prepared to effectively explain this position.

But it is important that your testimony not be shaped by the black-or-white, either-or oppositions found in the legal system. Be truthful, even though it may adversely affect the case of the attorney who called you as a witness. You cannot be faulted for believing in your opinions but, defensiveness to the point of withholding information is unacceptable. Acknowledge the limits of your expertise in a given area. Don't be reluctant to take time to consider a question, or to say, "I don't know." One can better say "I don't know" with qualifications such as "That question presupposes a knowledge of internal medicine, an area in which I have not been trained". Many legal critics of the psychological witness dismiss the credibility of "experts" who stretch psychological theory to reach a polarized conclusion. Honest, unbiased testimony will maintain your personal integrity, as well as that of the profession.

In court, dress and act conservatively, politely, pleasantly, and professionally. Speak loudly and clearly, and address the judge as "Your Honor" and the attorneys as "Mr. Smith" or "Ms. Jones". When responding to questions, begin by looking at the questioning attorney. As you continue, you can casually move your gaze in order to also address the judge or jury.

Be open about prior contacts with attorneys and any fees you are receiving. You have nothing to hide. The attorney cross-examining you may use frustrating legal tactics to disturb your composure and thereby devalue your testimony. Don't allow yourself to be provoked into arguing or losing your temper. Do not answer with a question of your own (unless you don't understand the question), and don't volunteer information beyond the bounds of the question or your knowledge. Take all questions seriously and, above all, retain your objectivity.

SUMMARY

For the uninformed, unprepared family therapist venturing for the first time into the no-man's land of the judicial system the experience has often been traumatic. A basic understanding of the legal process and proper preparation are of utmost importance. Pre-trial preparation is the key in transforming the family therapist into a poised, confident, objective, and valuable expert witness. Family therapists can provide valuable information to aid judge and juries in the difficult process of dealing with intrafamily sexuality. The family therapist who becomes familiar with the legal system and who becomes adequately prepared can find courtroom involvement to be a satisfying experience, as well as an added dimension to his/her professional role.

REFERENCES

Bartol, C.R. (1983). *Psychology and American Law*. Belmont, CA. Wadsworth Publishing Co.

Bauer, H. (1983). Preparation of the sexually abused child for court testimony. *Bulletin of the American Academy of Psychiatry and the Law, 11*, 287–289.

Blau, T. (1984). *The Psychologist As Expert Witness*. New York: Wiley.

Brodsky, S.L. (1977). The mental health professional on the witness stand: A survival guide. In B.D. Sales (Ed.), *Psychology in the legal process*. New York: Spectrum.

Chamberlain, M., Krell, H., & Preis, K. (1982). Legal aspects of child neglect. *The American Journal of Forensic Psychiatry, 3*, 151–158.

Derdeyn, A.L. (1975). Child custody consultation. *American Journal of Orthopsychiatry, 45*, 791–801.

Ennis, B.G. & Litwack, T.R. (1974). Psychiatry and the presumption of expertise: Flipping coins in the courtroom. *California Law Review, 62*, 693.

Fraser, B.G. (1981). "Sexual child abuse: the legislation and the law in the United States." in Mrazek & Kempe (eds.), *Sexually abused children and their families*. New York: Pergammon Press, 55–73.

Goldzband, M.G. (1982). *Consulting in child custody*. Lexington, MA: Lexington Books.

Goulett, H.M. (1965). *The insanity defense in criminal trials*. St. Paul, Minnesota: West Publishing Co.

Hyde, M.L., & Kaufman, P.A. (1984). Women molested as children: Therapeutic and legal issues in civil actions. *American Journal of Forensic Psychiatry, 5*, 147–157.

Johnson, S., & Blazer, D. (1980). Sex offenses: A short questionnaire assessing knowledge and attitudes. *The Bulletin of the American Academy of Psychiatry and the Law, 8*, 280–287.

Johnston, M.S.K. (1976). "The sexually mistreated child: Diagnostic evaluation," in *Child Abuse and Neglect*, Vol. 3, U.S. Dept. of Health, Education, and Welfare, Office of Human Development, Wash. D.C.: U.S. Government Printing office, 943–949.

Kurlychek, R.T. & DeHeer, N.D. (1982). Court testimony by mental health professionals in corrections: Considerations and guidelines for effective involvement. *Corrective and Social Psychiatry, 28*, 137–139.

Litwack, T.R., Gerber, G.L., & Fenster, C.A. (1979). The proper role of psychology in child custody disputes. *Journal of Family Law, 18*, 269–300.

Marin, B.V., Holmes, D.L., Guth, M., & Kovac, P. (1979). The potential of children as eye-witnesses. *Law and Human Behavior, 3*, 295–306.

Mrazek, P.B. & Kempe, C.H. (eds.) (1981). *Sexually Abused Children and Their Families*. New York: Pergammon Press.

Nichols, J.F. (1980). The marital/family therapist as an expert witness: Some thoughts and suggestions. *Journal of Marital & Family Therapy, 6*, 293–299.

Sgroi, S.M. (1982). *Handbook of clinical intervention in child sexual abuse*. Lexington, MA: Lexington Press.

Trepper, T.S. & Traicoff, M.E. (1983). Treatment of intrafamily sexuality: Issues in therapy and research. *Journal of Sex Education and Therapy, 9*, 14–18.

Wells, D.M. (1983). "Expert testimony: To admit or not to admit." *Florida Bar Journal, 57*, 672–676.

Woody, R.H. (1977). Behavioral science criteria in child custody determinations. *Journal of Marriage and Family Counseling, 3*, 11–18.

Ziskin, J. (1981). *Coping with psychiatric and psychological testimony*, (3rd ed.) Volume I. Venice, CA: Law and Psychology Press. (a)

Ziskin, J. (1981). *Coping with psychiatric and psychological testimony*, (3rd ed.) Volume II. Venice, CA: Law and Psychology Press. (b)

Sexual Abuse and the Family: A Critical Analysis

Jon R. Conte

INTRODUCTION

Family oriented perspectives and intervention approaches are currently quite popular among mental health professionals. With increasing professional interest in sexual abuse of children, it is natural that "family" models should be applied to understanding and treating the problem of adult sexual use of children. Supporting this interest is a body of professional literature, much of it developed over the last twenty-five years which is referenced time and time again as indicating a connection between various characteristics of families and sexual abuse of children.

A considered conceptual and empirical review of the ideas which form the essential components of the "family" perspectives on child sexual abuse, suggest a number of significant limitations of such ideas as they have been formulated to date. This paper offers such a review in the belief that the potential utility of a "family" perspectives can only be realized if such perspectives are based more firmly on conceptual frameworks and empirical findings which are consistent with each other. Specifically, this paper will suggest that the connection between characteristics of families and sexual abuse of children has not been established, that much of the literature used to suggest such a connection is weak, and that the family connection as currently conceptualized lacks substantial support. The paper reviews preliminary evidence which raises question about the family's role in sexual abuse of children, identifies a number of ways that current "family-oriented" thinking may be harmful to abused children, and suggests directions for family-oriented research and intervention in the future.

SUPPORTING LITERATURE

Sexual abuse in families has been referred to as the "perverse triangle" in which an adult forms a cross-generational (e.g., father-

Portions of this paper were delivered at the Second National Conference on the Sexual Victimization of Children, Washington, D.C., May 6–8, 1982.

Jon R. Conte, Ph.D., is an Assistant Professor, School of Social Service Administration, University of Chicago, 969 E. 60th St., Chicago, Illinois 60637.

daughter) coalition against the same-age peer (Rist, 1979). A commonly described dynamic finds the daughter assuming many of her mother's domestic roles (e.g., cooking dinner, supervising younger siblings). Already poor marital relations deteriorate further until sexual relations between the father and mother completely cease as a result of some situational factor (e.g., mother has a new baby or temporarily is absent from the home). The father, who is unwilling to act out sexually outside of the family, turns sexually to the daughter who has already stepped into many of her mother's duties. Fear of family disintegration and abandonment motivates all three of the participants in a pathological system in which sexual abuse becomes a tension-reduction mechanism maintaining the integrity of the family (Kaufman, Peck, and Tagiuri, 1954; Lustig, Dresser, Spellman, and Murray, 1966).

For the fathers, incest becomes a means of projecting the hostility felt toward their own mothers who had abandoned them as children and for fulfilling through a liaison with their daughter the Oedipal liaison denied them as children (Cavallin, 1966; Lustig et al., 1966). The fathers are described as inadequate, weak, or dependent; coming from early family histories of parental abandonment, harshness, or punitive child rearing; insecure and inadequate in interpersonal relationships, especially heterosexual relationships; underachievers in family, social, and occupational roles; markedly diminished sensitivity to others; and chronically anxious and dependent (Cavallin, 1966; Groth, Hobson, and Gary, 1982; Lustig et al., 1966; Panton, 1979; Rist, 1979; Swanson, 1968; Weiner, 1964). Overpowering feeling of inadequacy, dependency, and anxiety become disguised as genital urges and are directed toward those in the family least capable of retaliation (their daughters) as relief from the fear of abandonment (Gutheil and Avery, 1977). Old Oedipal strivings and hostility toward the father's mother become rekindled by relationships with a withdrawing and cold wife and are given unconscious expression through incest (Cavallin, 1966).

Most frequently, the incestuous mother is seen as the "cornerstone of the pathological family system" (Bastani and Kantsmith, 1980; Brant and Tisza, 1977). These mothers are described as having poor relationships with their own mothers, whom they see as stern, demanding, controlling, cold, hostile, and rejecting (Kaufman et al., 1954). The mother singles out one of her daughters (usually the oldest) to psychologically replace the mother's own mother. The daughter is then indulged materially and expected to assume emotional responsibility for her own mother (who in turn acts out her anger at her mother substitute (her daughter) by pushing her into bed with the father) (Kaufman et al., 1954). This also serves to relieve the mother of sexual pressure from the father (Gutheil and Avery, 1977; Machotoka, Pittman, and Flomenhaft, 1967). Similarly, for the incest victim, the father becomes a weapon against the mother who is seen as cruel, unjust, and depriving (Machotoka et al., 1967).

There are a number of elements in this view which are characteristic of a family perspective generally. These include: the importance of a multi-generational view in understanding problems; the notion that the problem (sexual abuse) is symptomatic of a dysfunctional family in which every member of the family contributes to the development and maintenance of the problem; and the belief that the problem (symptom) may not in itself have significance, but rather have a meaning within the family which is not readily apparent in the behavior (e.g., sexual abuse as a tension-reduction mechanism or as a means of displacing feelings of isolation).

AREAS OF WEAKNESS

This literature reflects a number of significant weaknesses. Were it not for the fact that it is referenced frequently in current literature as an authoritative source for various statements about the connection between sexual abuse of children and families, it would be possible to overlook these weaknesses as products of a different age when standards were less rigorous. However, since this is not possible, it is important to look at some of the major weaknesses.

Virtually all of the literature describes small samples of sexual abuse cases. Most are clinical descriptions, unaided by any kind of measurement or control procedures. There is no way to determine to how many cases a specific observation actually applies nor how accurate statements actually are. Many of the articles were written at a time when few cases of sexually abused children were identified and those which were known to professionals were often incest cases. These factors raise questions about how representative the cases described in this literature are to the large number of child sexual abuse cases currently being identified. More importantly, the literature lacks the kind of scientific support (e.g., estimates of the reliability of statements) which current standards require before much weight is given to statements about clinical phenomena.

Also, it is not clear why so much energy has gone into speculating about intrafamily sexual abuse (which usually means father/stepfather-daughter incest). Although there has been some discussion of other types of sexual abuse (see, e.g., father-son incest [Dixon, Arnold, and Calestro, 1978]), the bulk of literature has focused on father-daughter incest, which is a small proportion of the total victim population. Data reported by Conte and Berliner (1981) on a sample of 583 sexually abused children indicate that 32% of the cases involved the father or stepfather as the offender). It would seem that clinical practice should be based upon knowledge which applies to the largest number of cases first and then variations in types of cases identified.

Much of the family literature has assumed a priori that incest is fundamentally different from other types of cases in which children are sexually victimized. For example, much of the literature has the implicit belief that fathers who sexually abuse their children are significantly different from other adults who sexually use children. To the contrary, there is preliminary evidence indicating that incestuous and nonincestuous child molesters share more in common than there is that separates them. A number of authors describe a similar type of person who commits sexual offenses against children. They are seen as dependent, inadequate individuals with early histories characterized by conflict, disruption, abandonment, abuse, and exploitation (see e.g., Groth et al., 1983 or Swanson, 1968). Panton (1979) compared the MMPI profiles of incestuous offenders and nonincestuous child sex offenders and found common features, including feelings of insecurity, inadequacy in interpersonal relationships, dependency, and early family histories characterized by social isolation and family discord. The only significant difference was that the nonincestuous offenders functioned at a lower level of sexual maturity.

Part of the belief that intrafamily sexual abuse is different than extrafamily sexual abuse is the belief that incestuous fathers tend not to involve children outside of their family as sexual objects, and the incestuous behavior begins as husband-wife sexual contact terminates. Although representative data are lacking, there is evidence to suggest that the pattern is more complex than this. In fact, there is great variation in whether men have exclusive or multiple sexual relations with their daughters, other children outside the home, and their wives. For example, Josiassen, Fantuzzo, and Rosen (1980) report on the case of a thirty-seven year old man who had pedophilic experiences during a time which he was also having sexual relations with his wife. Marshall (1979) reports on the case of a thirty-three year old male arrested for sexual relations with the thirteen year old daughter of a neighbor family and who continued having sexual intercourse with his wife (approximately three times a week). Although this offender never abused his own children, he abused approximately twenty-five young girls over a six-year period. More importantly, data generated by Gene Abel and Judith Becker at their clinic in New York suggest that the pattern of types of deviancy incestuous fathers present is quite complex. Of the 142 men referred to their clinic for sexually abusing a daughter, in treatment it was learned that 44% had been abusing female children outside the home while incestuously involved with a daughter. Eleven percent had also been abusing male children and 18% raping adult women (Abel, 1983).

SYSTEMS ECOLOGICAL PERSPECTIVE

Another problem with much of the literature supporting a family perspective is its focus on the psychological development and functioning of individuals (largely father or stepfather and mother of the victim). It is believed that each individual in the family makes a contribution to a pathological system in which family dynamics serve to maintain the sexual abuse and the functioning, albeit pathological, of the family as a unit. With rare exception (see e.g., Mrazek and Bentovim, 1981), little has been written from a family systems perspective about sexual abuse and families. However, it is a perspective popular in practice settings.

Several aspects of a family systems perspective applied to sexual abuse of children deserve consideration. For example, some practitioners seem to believe that the presence of a symptom (problem) in one part of the system explains its presence in another part or parts. One of the common notions in the clinical lore which has developed around sexual abuse, is that a large percentage of the mothers of sexually abused children were themselves abused as children. Although there are no descriptive reports of how widespread this phenomenon is, clinical experience does indicate that this is a characteristic in some cases. The point here is that this observation, when it is true in a particular case, constitutes a specific descriptive truism and not a causal statement. Systems theory is a general theory describing the functioning of systems; it is not a causal theory, and in the previous example, nothing has been explained by the observation that in some families mothers and their children are both victims of sexual abuse. It is not clear what accounts for this apparent relationship or indeed whether the relationship exists at all. One might wonder if the observation is simply a function of the great numbers of women and children who are victims of sexual abuse.

A family perspective applied to sexual abuse has only begun its task at a stage of descriptive identification of variables which characterize families in which sexual abuse takes place. The next and more important step is to identify the processes which account for the development of sexual abuse. For example, even if it were true that there is a relationship between a child's sexual abuse and the fact that her mother were also victimized, what seems important is to identify what mechanisms within the family or elsewhere account for this relationship. Do mothers who were abused as children, create implicit expectations (that all children are abused) which children somehow learn and act on? Or do mothers abused as children place their children in situations with high risk for victimization because of their own need to relive their own childhood experiences?

It is not at all clear how widespread many of the supposed characteristics of sexually abusing families actually are. For example, role reversal between child victims and their mothers is often said to be nearly universal (see e.g., Thorman, 1983). And yet, when Conte (1985) made an effort to actually measure the presence of role reversal in incest cases (N = 66), he found that 32% of clinic sample of incest cases had no indication of role reversal at all and that the number of indicators of role reversal varied greatly over the remaining cases. Another problem with many of the "family" characteristics of sexual abuse cases, is that they tend to describe what is generally obvious in these cases. For example, to suggest that power is not equal in incestuous families (Thorman, 1983) or that the boundary between parent and child has been destroyed when a father has sex with his daughter is to point out the obvious. These characteristics are often mentioned as if they had some role in the development of incestuous behavior. In fact, the relationship between these characteristics and incest has not been demonstrated. Nor in fact, has the actual presence of these characteristics in many families been established.

Another simplistic application of systems theory to sexual abuse and families results from a premature determination of what the relevant "system" is. Focusing attention on the nuclear family in which a stepfather or father sexually abuse a daughter may have resulted in a failure to use a family perspective to critically examine other potentially important systems. For example, the family which may tell us most about sexual abuse is the sex offender's family of origin. It is prudent to remember that it increasingly appears that many adults who sexually abuse children began this behavior when they were young, long before they entered the family in which they abused their own daughter. Judith Becker and Gene Abel indicate that about 60% of the adults in their clinic began abusing children when they were themselves adolescents (Abel and Becker, 1983). An examination of families across a sample of offenders who abuse children who are related and not related to them may tell us more about the problem. It may also be fruitful to examine the nature of relationships between families in which sex offenders live and/or families in which children are sexually abused with the wider ecological system of which they are part. For example, a number of authors have speculated that a relationship exists between sexism in the society and sexual abuse (see e.g., Butler, 1980; Herman and Hirschman, 1977; McIntyre, 1981; Stevens, 1980); others have speculated that child pornography acts as a disinhibitor to sexual use of children (Finkelhor, 1985). These and other variables which may be related to the development of sexual abuse (e.g., isolation) require a critical examination of the family and the other systems which interact with it.

Additionally, a systems theory view of sexual abuse and families would seem to suggest the importance of viewing the individual family member as a system made up of various subsystems. These include cognitive, emotional, behavioral, and physiological systems. Examination of the contribution of these various subsystems to the development and maintenance of sexual abuse may be profitable. For example, a systemic view of sexual offenders directs attention toward a number of variables, some historical (e.g., punitive child-rearing experiences) and some contemporary which describe the current life functioning of men who sexually use children. These contemporary influences include cognitive distortions which provide excuses for sexual use of children (e.g., "I was only teaching her about sex") and learned behaviors which are emotionally and physically reinforced (e.g., sexual arousal to children). It appears that many clinicians emphasize family process variables over other potentially powerful systemic ones.

One of the most problematic aspects of some applications of systems thinking to these cases, is the notion that the problem isn't what it appears but rather something else. As translated in these cases, this means that the sexual abuse isn't really sexual at all. The adult who sexually abuses children is giving sexual expression to non-sexual needs. The specific nature of the needs vary by the clinical theory used to describe the behavior, but they include: the need for closeness, anger or hostility, the creation of a secret which will maintain the family unit, the need of closeness, or the need to have revenge against the same age peer.

There are a number of problems with this notion. Virtually all sexuality, deviant and nondeviant, contains both sexual and non-sexual dimensions. Indeed, one of the mental health implications of sexuality is that it can be a means of expressing anger, closeness, dependence, caring, or affirmation. There is no reason to assume that sexual abuse of children does not include sexual and non-sexual dimensions. Additionally, there is increasing evidence gathered through the use of physiological assessments of sexual arousal that incestuous and non-incestuous men are in fact both sexually aroused to children (see e.g., Abel, Becker, Murphy, and Flanagan, 1981).

INTERVENTION LIMITATIONS

Although there is not currently available a systematic study of the application of these ideas to practice some of these "family" beliefs can result in problems in intervening in these cases. To the extent that these ideas make it possible to shift responsibility for sexual abuse away from the adult who initiates and maintains sexual contact with children by suggesting that it is a result of mechanisms operating within the family (not the individual), these ideas support the very pathology which they seek to change. Adults who have sex with children develop elaborate rationalization (e.g., "It's better that she learn about sex from me, rather than on the streets") which make it possible to psychologically deny or minimize what they do. An essential initial treatment issue with adults who have sex with children is helping them to accept responsibility for their own behavior by viewing it for the abusive behavior it is. Any other treatment stance is collusive with the client's problem.

Similarly, not treating the problem, at least in part, as a sexual one, is to not directly help the client with the problem which places him at legal and social jeopardy. Therapy may be very successful in altering many of the conditions potentially associated with sexual use of children (e.g., denial, poor self concept, diminished social skills) and still not address the problem in its sexual dimension. This can mean that some men will leave therapy still unable to control their fantasies which involve children as sexual objects and still sexually aroused to children. Such men are treatment failures waiting to be identified for abusing children after termination of treatment.

From a child victim's perspective, family oriented intervention can also be problematic. For example, as Hare-Mustin (1981) has pointed out, many traditional family therapists tend to support tradition, sex-role stereotyped power distributions in families. When parental power has been used to coerce or manipulate a child into a sexual relationship, fundamental alterations in parent power would seem to be necessary. More importantly, family perspectives which see the entire family as a group make it virtually impossible that the child victim will report incidents of sexual abuse during treatment. In this way, the family therapist acts in collusion with the abusing father. Additionally, family group intervention can assume a decision that the family should stay together which individual family members might best make before family intervention is begun. Also, to the extent that the therapists holds beliefs that minimize what happened to the victim by believing that the problem is really something else and directing therapy time toward the "real" problem, the therapist can further traumatize the victim by ignoring her abuse and pain.

SUMMARY

This paper has argued that the connection between characteristics of family's and sexual abuse of child family members is without current empirical support. While there is no single family perspective and there is as much diversity within family perspectives as there is between family and individually oriented views of human behavior, still taken as a whole "family" perspectives tend to share a common view of sexual abuse of children. Much of the literature often used to support this view is methodologically weak and actually tends to describe the pathology of individual family members.

Interventions based upon many "family" ideas about sexual abuse can be destructive to victimized children and often appear to be ineffective in helping individuals who sexually abuse children control their behavior. This charge should not obscure the fact that individual clinicians using some of these ideas do in fact do excellent clinical work with sexual abuse cases. Also, some cases may in fact look very much like the case described in some of the family literature. Most importantly, as Sgroi (1982) has pointed out, virtually all sexual abuse of children involves a child's family. This involvement varies from cases in which a family member abuses the child to cases in which the family shares with the child the impact of the child's abuse. Concern for and working with a victim's family is an essential component of clinical intervention in these cases.

This paper argues that work with the child victim's family must recognize that the role of the family in the etiology of sexual abuse of children is assumptive and lacks strong empirical support. The presence of any of the characteristics of "abusive families" described in the literature should not be assumed a priori but should be identified in a clinical assessment. When present, these characteristics (e.g., mother/daughter role reversal) should be the target of intervention. It should also be clear that the presence of such a characteristic may be the result of sexual abuse not causal of such abuse.

For the time, greater progress in developing treatment models may be made, if the role of the family in the etiology of childhood sexual victimization is put aside. In time research may be available which more directly addresses this issue. It may be helpful to apply a family perspective in treatment of cases: as long as such a perspective makes no a priori assumptions which limit the dimensions of human functioning the clinician assesses and targets for change. For example, awareness that sexual abuse of children is a complex clinical problem involving, at least in part, sexual arousal and sexual fantasies involving children, may be incorporated into family oriented treatment approach. Similarly, recognition that sexual abuse of children by fathers inherently involves abuse of parental power can be incorporated into a family perspective in which alinement of parental power is one of the treatment goals.

FUTURE DIRECTIONS

There are a number of directions for future family-oriented research and treatment development. These include:

1) Expand the Family Perspective to All Cases of Sexual Abuse

A family or systemic perspective should direct attention toward a number of variables which may be associated with sexual abuse (see number 3 below). Research investigating the relationship between these variables and sexual abuse may determine the degree to which intra- and extrafamily sexual abuse represent similar or dissimilar phenomena. This perspective should be applied through research to all types of cases and variation by type of case empirically identified. Treatment implications of such variation could subsequently be identified.

2) Expand the Range of Systems Which Are Included

It is wholly consistent with a systemic perspective to regard individuals, dyads of individuals, the family as a whole, and other naturally occurring groups in the family's ecological environment as systems. A search for variables which explain the development and maintenance of sexual abuse of children should identify variables in each of these subsystems which are potentially related to sexual abuse and compare these variables in relation to each other to identify those across systems which have the greatest explanatory power. To date, there is no evidence to suggest that one system or any set of variables is more important in understanding sexual abuse. Such an undertaking is within the methodological capability of research, given investigators who are willing to apply a systemic view in identifying potentially important variables. In this regard, work integrating intra-individual systems (e.g., sexual arousal, cognitions which serve to minimize or distort behavior, and emotional needs) with extra-individual systems (e.g., family developed expectations about victimization or attitudes toward sexual expression) would seem to be quite promising.

The belief that all important processes originate in and take place between family members is a distortion of systems theory. The family is both a system of systems (e.g., individuals, dyads, and triads in interaction) and a system within a larger ecological environment. Understanding sexual abuse may require a larger systematic perspective which accounts for the influence of various systems in the development and maintenance of sexual use of children. It may well be that there are a number of very different reasons why sexual abuse of children takes place. This will not be known, however, if we prematurely limit our attention to sexual abuse taking place in one type of family system.

3) Identify the Processes Associated With the Development and/or the Maintenance of Sexual Abuse

Systems theory points to the importance of transactional patterns between systems as significant variables in determining the behavior of systems. Family systems theory has identified a number of processes within families which *may be* associated with sexual abuse. Although these processes have largely been untested, they do suggest potential areas for research to investigate the means by which sexual abuse is developed and maintained. These include:

—The function of sexual abuse. An analysis of the result (payoffs) of sexual abuse for various individuals and the family unit as a whole may be helpful in understanding the functions the abuse serves within the family and the consequences that help to maintain it. It is a common tenet of the family perspective that the meaning of behavior may best be understood when it is seen within the context of ongoing interaction between family members. For example, Patterson (1979) has demonstrated that the aggressive behavior of some children may function to obtain attention from parents which normal children obtain through prosocial behaviors. In some families, sexual abuse of children is only one of any number of ways that individual family members use and hurt each other. In some of these families, sexual abuse may reflect the control the father exercises over all family members. In others, it seems to reflect a pattern of behavior learned in the father's family of origin. An understanding of the function that the sexual abuse serves for every member of the family, if such a function exists at all, will require research looking at both individual and family variables.

—Family myths, secrets, themes, belief systems. There has been considerable attention applied to the perceptions, or beliefs, which members of a family share in common (see e.g., Karpel, 1980; Reiss, 1979; Sederer and Sederer, 1979). These common cognitive sets may function as mediators for sexual abuse, either eliciting certain kinds of behavior, providing a rationalization for other kinds of behavior, or preventing or suppressing alternative behaviors. Some themes which are often identified in cases of sexual abuse include: isolation, victimization, and sexist attitudes. Families in which a prevailing theme is that family members are sexually victimized may communicate to its members the inevitability that children will be the victims of sexual assault. While knowledge has not yet been developed which fully accounts for the processes through which such a theme leads to sexual victimization of children, identification through controlled research that such themes exist could be an important first step.

One of the greatest difficulties the search for family processes associated with sexual abuse must deal with is how to differentiate between processes which are responsible for the development or generation of sexual abuse (primary); those which only support or help maintain sexual abuse (secondary); or those which are a consequence of sexual abuse (Minuchin, Baker, Rosman, Liebman, Milman, and Todd, 1975). These distinctions are crucial if we are to understand the differences between those processes which are responsible for the development of sexual abuse versus those processes which are a consequence of sexual abuse within the family. For example, is an enmeshed relationship between father and daughter the cause of sexual abuse or a natural consequence of a father's sexual use of his daughter?

It may be some time before the actual mechanisms of transmission are discovered between case characteristics (e.g., prior sexual victimization) and behavior (e.g., sexually abusing children). However, for the time it is sufficient to identify those characteristics of cases which are common across types of child sexual abuse and those which vary.

4) *In Large Part, These Answers Will Come About Only as a Product of Research Efforts*

It is surprising that the family perspective as expressed currently has forgotten that the family perspective was developed initially as a research effort (Broderick and Schrader, 1981). To understand the role of families in sexual abuse of children will require research along a number of dimensions. These should include descriptive studies which seek characteristics which discriminate families in which sexual abuse takes place from other families. This effort may be more productive if there is not a premature reduction in the types of families or range of characteristics which are sought. Multivariate techniques make it feasible to take a systematic view in the search for variables which in isolation or interaction with each other are associated with sexual abuse. Such an effort should also distinguish between the presence of common case characteristics (e.g., several-generation history of victimization) and the actual processes which explain the presence of such a characteristic.

5) *Emphasize Treatment Research*

Very little attention has been focused to date on how to successfully intervene in cases in which a child has been sexually abused. Given the large number of human lives involved in these cases, some attention should be directed toward understanding how treatment influences their situation. Outcome studies documenting the differential success of alternative treatment approaches are certainly needed. Additionally, studies describing the kinds of problems clients and therapists encounter in resolving this problem could also be quite helpful in treatment and social policy discussion. For example, what are the consequences to victims and adults of involving versus not involving the justice system, or when families are seen only in family groups what are the consequences for child victims and others in the family?

REFERENCES

Abel, G.G., Becker, J.V., Murphy, W.D., & Flanagan, B. 1981. Identifying dangerous child molesters. In R.B. Stuart (Ed.), *Violent Behavior: Social Learning Approaches to Prediction, Management and Treatment,* New York: Brunner/Mazel.

Abel, Gene. 1983. Treatment of the sexual offender. Lecture delivered at Treatment of Sex Offenders: Fact or Fiction, Issac Ray Center, Chicago, September 30, 1983.

Abel, Gene and Becker, Judith. 1983. Assessing and Treating Sexual Offenders. Paper presented at World Congress of Behavior Therapy, Washington, D.C., December.

Barton, C. and Alexander, J. 1981. Functional family therapy. In Handbook of family therapy, A. Gorman and D. Kniskern, eds. Brunner/Mazel, New York, pp. 403–443.

Basini, J. and Kentsmith, D. 1980. Psychotherapy with wives of sexual deviants. American Journal of Psychotherapy. 24(1):20–25.

Brant, R. and Tisza, V. 1977. The sexually misused child. American Journal of Orthopsychiatry. 47(1):80–90.

Broderick, C. and Schrader, S. 1981. This history of professional marriage and family therapy. In Handbook of family therapy, A. Gorman and D. Kniskern, eds. Brunner/Mazel, New York, pp. 5–25.

Butler, S. 1980. Incest: Whose reality, whose theory? Aegis. Summer/Autumn, 48–55.

Cavallin, H. 1966. Incestuous fathers: A clinical report. American Journal of Psychiatry. 122(10):1132–1138.

Conte, J. and Berliner, L. 1981. Sexual abuse of children: Implications for practice. Social Casework. 63(10):601–606.

Conte, Jon R. 1985. The effects of sexual abuse on children: Preliminary findings unpublished paper available from author at School of Social Service Administration, 969 East 60th St., Chicago, Illinois, 60637.

Dixon, K., Arnold, L. and Calestro, K. 1978. Father-son incest: Underreported psychiatric problem? American Journal of Psychiatry. 135(7):835–838.

Finkelhor, D. 1979. Sexually victimized children. Free Press, New York.

Finkelhor, D. 1985. Child sexual abuse: New theories and research. Free Press, New York.

Groth, A., Hobson, W. and Gary, T. 1982. The child molester: Clinical observations. Social Work and Child Sexual Abuse. 1(1/2):129–144.

Gutheil, T. and Avery, N. 1977. Multiple overt incest as family defense against loss. Family Process. 16(1):105–116.

Hare-Mustin, R. 1981. A feminist approach to family therapy. In E. Howell and M. Bayes, eds. Women and mental health. Basic Books, New York.

Herman, J. and Hirschman, L. 1977. Father-Daughter incest. Journal of Woman in Culture and Society. 2(4):735–756.

Josiassen, R., Fantuzzo, J. and Rosen, A. 1980. Treatment of pedophilia using multistage aversion therapy with social skills training. Journal of Behavior Therapy and Experimental Psychiatry. 11(2):55–61.

Karpel, M. 1980. Family secrets. Family Process. 295–306.

Kaufman, I., Peck, A. and Tagiuri, C. 1954. The family constellation and overt incestuous relations between father and daughter. American Journal of Orthopsychiatry, 24(2):266–279.

Lustig, N., Dresser, J., Spellman, S. and Murray, T. 1966. Incest: A family group survival pattern. Archives of General Psychiatry. 14(1):31–40.

Machotoka, P., Pittman, F. and Flomenhaft, S. 1967. Incest as a family affair. Family Process. 6(1):98–116.

Marshall, W. 1979. Satiation therapy: A procedure for reducing deviant sexual arousal. Journal of Applied Behavior Analysis. 12(3):377–389.

Mrazek, P. and Bentovim, A. 1981. Incest and the dysfunctional family system. In P. Mrazek and C. Kempe, eds., Sexually abused children and their families. Pergamon Press, New York.

McIntyre, K. 1981. Role of mothers in father-daughter incest: A feminist analysis. Social Work. 26(6):462–467.

Minuchin, S., Baker, L., Rosman, B., Liebman, R., Milman, L. and Todd, T. 1975. A conceptual model of psychosomatic illness in children. Archives of General Psychiatry. 32:1031–1038.

Panton, J. 1979. MMPI profile configurations associated with incestuous and non-incestuous child molesters. Psychological Reports. 45(1):335–338.

Patterson, G. 1979. The aggressive child: Victim and architect of coercive system. In Behavior modification and families, E. Marsh, L. Hamerlynch, and L. Handy, eds. Brunner/Mazel, New York, pp. 267–316.

Quinsey, V. L., Chaplin, T. C., and Carrigan, M. F. 1979. Sexual preferences among incestuous and nonincestuous child molesters. Behavior Therapy. 10:562–565.

Reiss, D. 1981. The family's construction of reality. Harvard University Press, Cambridge, Massachusetts.

Revitch, E. and Weiss, R. 1962. The pedophilian offender. Diseases of the Nervous System. 23(2):73–78.

Rist, K. 1979. Incest: Theoretical and clinical views. American Journal of Orthopsychiatry. 49(4):630–691.

Sederer, L. and Sederer, N. 1979. A family myth: Sex therapy gone awry. Family Process. 18(3):315–321.

Sgroi, S. 1982. Handbook of clinical intervention in child sexual abuse. Lexington Books, Lexington, Mass.

Stevens, D. 1980. Dynamics of victimization. Paper presented at National Association of Social Workers 1st National Conference on Social Work Practice with Women, Washington, D.C., available from author at Sexual Assault Center, Horborrien Medical Center, Seattle, Washington.

Swanson, D. 1968. Adult sexual abuse of children. Diseases of the Nervous System. 29(10):677–683.

Thorman, G. 1982. Incestuous families. Charles Thomas, Springfield.

Weiner, I. 1964. On incest: A survey. Excerpta Criminology. 4(2):137–155.